Chefs of
the Triangle

Chefs of *the Triangle*

Their Lives, Recipes, and Restaurants

by Ann Prospero

Foreword by Moreton Neal

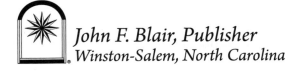

John F. Blair, Publisher
Winston-Salem, North Carolina

JOHN F. BLAIR
PUBLISHER
1406 Plaza Drive
Winston-Salem, North Carolina 27103
www.blairpub.com

Manufactured in the United States of America

All photos are by Ann Prospero unless otherwise noted.

COVER IMAGES
Clockwise from upper left are dishes by
Chef Colin Bedford at Fearrington House Restaurant,
Chef Jim Anile at Revolution, Chef Sarig Agasi at Zely & Ritz,
and Chef Michael Chuong at Ân.

Library of Congress Cataloging-in-Publication Data

Prospero, Ann.
  Chefs of the Triangle : their lives, recipes, and restaurants / by Ann Prospero ; foreword by Moreton Neal.
     p.   cm.
  Includes index.
  ISBN 978-0-89587-370-5 (pbk. : alk. paper)
  1. Cooks--North Carolina--Research Triangle Park Region--Biography.
  2. Restaurants--North Carolina--Research Triangle Park Region. 3. Cookery.
  I. Title.
  TX649.A1P76 2009
  641.5092'2--dc22
  [B]
                        2009025849

www.blairpub.com
DESIGN BY DEBRA LONG HAMPTON

To Michael

Contents

Foreword

Ann Prospero's book couldn't be timelier. *Chefs of the Triangle: Their Lives, Recipes, and Restaurants* offers an insider's view of Triangle restaurant kitchens just as the national food media has spotlighted the area, making stars of our chefs and gastro-tourist destinations of our restaurants and farmers' markets. Dubbed "the foodiest town in America" by *Bon Appétit*, Chapel Hill/Durham now has its own culinary bus tour!

Those of us who are fortunate enough to live and eat here realize how blessed we are. But it wasn't always like that.

Back in 1972 when Bill Neal and I arrived in Chapel Hill for graduate school, the restaurant pickings were slim. In this part of the world, most eateries were standard steakhouses, fish camps, and pizzerias. The four conspicuous exceptions were the glamorous Danziger restaurants, flamboyant creations of the son of an Austrian candy maker. Our favorite was the exotic Villa Teo with its "continental" menu.

Bill and I loved to eat well but had no intention of becoming professional cooks. To make ends meet, however, we turned our passion for cooking to good use, catering parties for Bill's professors, using recipes from my grandmother and stacks of *Gourmet* magazines. Eventually, I found work at Hope Valley Country Club's kitchen with French chef Jacques Condoret, while Bill moonlighted making desserts at Chapel Hill Country Club.

Our relationship with the Condoret family and a growing addiction to Julia Child's books gave Bill a vision to be a "real" chef at a time when the term *Southern chef* was an oxymoron. He yearned to go to France for training but settled for a cooking job at the best restaurant in town—our old hangout, the Villa Teo. Under the tutelage of Chef Henry Schliff, Bill took to his new career. When Schliff left a year later, owner Bibi Danziger asked Bill to head the Villa's kitchen.

Culinary adventures in France opened up a new world for us. We developed a seasonal approach to cooking and by 1976 were ready to open our own place. Chapel Hill businessman R. B. Fitch, in the planning stages of an ambitious project that would become Fearrington Village, showed us the property's sizable farmhouse. We moved in and transformed the first floor into Restaurant La Résidence, the first fresh produce–oriented restaurant in the Triangle. (La Résidence no longer exists at Fearrington Village. It is now in Chapel Hill under new ownership.)

A few years later, Bill and partner Gene Hamer revamped an old West Franklin Street diner called Crook's Corner. The eatery caught the eye of Craig Claiborne, the powerful restaurant critic for the *New York Times*, who had already put La Résidence on the national culinary map with a glowing review. The legendary kingmaker showed up in our little town after Bill opened Crook's Corner. Claiborne encouraged Bill to focus on Southern dishes using fresh produce and classical French techniques. Bill went to work writing *Bill Neal's Southern Cooking*. Soon afterward, Crook's evolved into the South's answer to Chez Panisse, the pivotal California restaurant created by Alice Waters, the patron saint of American regional cuisine.

A natural teacher, Bill encouraged his protégées to think as much about the history and culture of each dish as about flavor combinations and techniques. "Crook's was an intellectually stimulating place to work," recalls former employee Amy Tornquist, now the owner of Watts Grocery. Robert Stehling of Hominy Grill in Charleston, South Carolina; John Currence of City Grocery in Oxford, Mississippi; and two of this book's subjects, Bill Smith and Tornquist, remember staff meals when Bill urged the fledgling cooks to develop their palates and think about creative uses of ingredients. Bill would have been proud that Stehling was awarded the James Beard Award for Best Chef in the Southeast in 2007; Currence received the Best Chef award in 2009.

Frank Stitt of the acclaimed Highlands Grill in Birmingham, Alabama, described Bill as "one of the first Southern chefs who had read and traveled widely, who possessed a sophisticated palate and applied that knowledge to a restaurant kitchen." Besides his virtuosity at the stove, Bill wrote books about Southern food and culture that helped earn him the nickname "the dean of Southern cuisine." He played an important role in destigmatizing the cooking profession in the South, elevating it from the ranks of servant to that of artist. He introduced into public venues many classic Southern dishes previously served only in homes and country clubs. And he improved these dishes by using only the freshest possible produce and herbs grown by local farmers.

Though Bill Neal and I established the Chapel Hill La Résidence in the French-Mediterranean style, it took a different direction when it changed ownership in 1992 and Chef Bill Smith and I left. Crook's Corner, still managed by original owner Gene Hamer, now has become an icon, the granddaddy of Southern regional restaurants. Bill Smith moved to Crook's kitchen in 1993, and his presence there proved a perfect fit. His own charming memoir/cookbook, *Seasoned in the South*, was published in 2005.

Ben and Karen Barker, who cooked alongside Bill Smith at La Résidence during the eighties, opened their own place, Magnolia Grill, now cited by *Gourmet* magazine as one of the fifty best restaurants in the country. Both Barkers have won James Beard Awards. Together, they wrote the cookbook *Not Afraid of Flavor*. Karen also wrote the tantalizing *Sweet Stuff*.

As you will discover in *Chefs of the Triangle*, Crook's Corner and La Résidence have influenced restaurants on the Chapel Hill/Durham side of the Triangle, but most of Raleigh's best chefs arrived here from other parts of the globe. You will learn about their training—some in local kitchens and others in prestigious culinary schools. Many have cooked at the best restaurants in the world and been mentored by such luminaries as Charlie Trotter, Emeril Lagasse, Patrick O'Connell, David Bouley, Jean-Georges Vongerichten, Tom Colicchio, and Jean-Louis Palladin.

Bill Neal raised consciousness about food and set a standard for restaurants in the Triangle. He planted seeds that, cultivated by his protégées and admirers, have blossomed into a garden of gastronomic delights. Yet without appreciative diners, the garden would not have thrived. In reality, it is the market—the diverse and sophisticated residents of the Triangle— who create and sustain the demand for excellent restaurants.

As *Raleigh Metro* magazine's food columnist, I have the privilege of sampling the best of our great bounty of restaurants. I know these chefs by their delicious work. And now, thanks to Ann Prospero, you and I are privy to the other side of the kitchen door—the backgrounds, inspirations, and dreams of these gifted culinary artists.

Moreton Neal

Acknowledgments

This book is the result of a conversation I had with my friend Michael Morton. I was telling him what I had learned about Bill Neal and the influence he had on other chefs when Michael said it would be great to have a book about the chefs in this area and their connections to one another. His idea became *Chefs of the Triangle.*

My friend Chef Dorette Snover, whom I knew first as an outstanding, evocative writer, led me gently through the complexities of a chef's life. I am deeply grateful to her. A graduate of the Culinary Institute of America, she has a superb cooking school, C'est Si Bon! She chooses to share what she knows with others rather than work in restaurants. I have had the opportunity to watch her work with adults and teens, showing them French cooking techniques through love, tenderness, and patience. This book includes three recipes for her "mother sauces," essential to the serious cook.

The recipes in this book have been tested and verified by a gracious and generous group of men and women. You can depend on the recipes working because of the cooking skills of these volunteers, among them foodies of all kinds—professors, deans, physicians, and other professionals, law students, graduate students, cooking school assistants, and so on. I am grateful to all of them for working so hard and to their friends and families, who ate what they made. Most of the recipes received rave reviews: "This will knock their socks off"; "This recipe has subtle, deep flavors"; "This was excellent. Really, really good"; "If all the recipes are this good, this book will be a bestseller." Clearly, the chefs presented me with some of their best ideas. I cannot express enough thanks to my volunteers: Sandra Ackerman, John Bowser, Carol Cantrell, Christina Demke, Angela Eberts, Matt Henry, Norman Keul, Dave Mackie, Jose Morales, Andrew D. Prins, Linda Prospero, Staci Rachman, Sarah Ribstein, Tim Stallmann, Amy Strong, Felicity Turner, Ingeborg Walther, Talia Wenzel, and Harrison O. Williams.

And lastly but not leastly, I offer special thanks to Carolyn Sakowski, Steve Kirk, Debbie Hampton, and Kim Byerly. I also thank Sharon Van Vechten and Jennifer Noble Kelly for their professional support.

Introduction

This small area of North Carolina, the Triangle, has undergone an explosive growth in imaginative chefs and restaurants. And it stems from a man most don't know a thing about—Bill Neal. His life has been chronicled by Moreton Neal in her memoir/cookbook *Remembering Bill Neal*. Bill Neal's enthusiasm for fresh, locally grown Southern foods made with French techniques propelled the region to discover, and then delight in, foods that were enchanting and exciting. Today, the Triangle boasts an abundance of creative chefs who feed on one another's energy. You'll read about them in this book. And you'll see connections you had no idea existed.

Chefs provide food that guests remember long after they've eaten, but the entire surroundings are part of the dining experience. The servers are trained, in effect, to give goodness to guests. Before guests taste the food, servers have tasted it and learned how it is made and what is in it. The ambience of a restaurant—its sounds, its colors, its lighting—is part of the event of dining out. Everything is designed to welcome, comfort, and amuse.

As you read these chapters, you'll begin to notice the connections. Bill Neal directly influenced Bill Smith and Amy Tornquist. Others were attracted to the area because chefs and their restaurants were thriving here, thanks to the revolution brought about by Bill Neal. Leading chefs such as Ben Barker, Karen Barker, and Scott Howell have influenced many others in the area and beyond. Chefs such as Shane Ingram, Walter Royal, and Andrea Reusing have also had a direct or indirect impact on many.

Two important players in the Triangle chef scene were R. B. Fitch and his late wife, Jenny. The Fitches knew Bill and Moreton Neal and invited them to open the first restaurant in Fearrington Village, which Fitch was about to build. Later, the Fitches were instrumental in inviting a young chef named Walter Royal to work with the legendary Edna Lewis at Fearrington House Restaurant. Royal is now executive chef at Angus Barn. And the Fitches invited Chefs Ben and Karen Barker to lead Fearrington House Restaurant. The Barkers later opened their own restaurant in Durham, Magnolia Grill.

Aaron Vandemark of Panciuto in Hillsborough spent critical months at Fearrington House learning that a chef can cut flowers from a garden out back and place them on a plate for dinner that night. And he spent months at Il Palio with Chef Ginaro Vilela learning the Italian cuisine that he would feature at his own restaurant. Jim Anile, who was chef at Il Palio for six years following Vilela, left to open his own restaurant, Revolution. And the current chef at Il Palio, Adam Rose, came to the area, he says, because it was a "hot spot for chefs."

The connections go on, a network of chefs supporting each other, sharing their knowledge, and competing in the Triangle.

Some are athletes. Sarig Agasi is a long-distance runner. Scott Howell is a golfer.

Some are artists. Vandemark, Alex Gallis, and Andres Macias are painters who consider themselves food artists for their work in the kitchen.

Some are graduates of culinary schools. Many went to the Culinary Institute of America, the leading school for chefs in North America. Amy Tornquist went abroad. Others studied at Johnson & Wales and a few at schools in California and Oregon. On the other hand, some chefs learned their craft by working with greats such as Emeril Lagasse, Charlie Trotter, Patrick O'Connell, David Bouley, Jean-Georges Vongerichten, and Edna Lewis, to name just a few.

Some chefs who believe that customers eat with their eyes take great pride in presenting beautifully structured and enticing plates. Others favor simplicity, believing that the quality of the food speaks for itself.

Many are perfectionists who will not let a plate leave the kitchen without first inspecting it to make sure it meets their standards.

All the chefs in this book make their breads and sausages and desserts—all their food, in fact—in house. Chip Smith gets up early to make the bread and desserts for dinner that night, for example. All the chefs use local produce and meats wherever possible, scouring the farmers' markets on weekends and Wednesdays. Amy Tornquist rises at six to go to two farmers' markets, one in Durham and one in Carrboro. Shane Ingram created his recipe for Fig Gazpacho because figs and tomatoes were abundant that day at the farmers' market. And farmers deliver their goods to the restaurants. The result is that the menus change weekly or even daily, depending on what farmers bring and what is available at the farmers' markets. And when local products are not available or are not plentiful enough, the chefs order the very best, often having it flown in.

Most of the chefs in this book run white-tablecloth restaurants. Many have received prestigious awards. All have won praise from local restaurant critics as well as from national media. They have received prestigious awards from the likes of the James Beard Foundation and *Gourmet*. Many own their restaurants or are part-owners. All provide extraordinary dining events.

The "Chefs' Chefs" section of the book includes leading chefs Ben Barker, Karen Barker, and Andrea Reusing, often referred to by other area chefs as models for their craft. Here, too, are recipes from a master of French techniques, Dorette Snover.

This book celebrates all the grand chefs who make the Triangle a mecca of delectable and memorable food, an area that has been recognized by the *New York Times, Gourmet, Bon Appétit, Saveur, Food & Wine*, and other national, regional, and local publications such as *Raleigh Metro* and the *Raleigh News & Observer*. You can participate in the chefs' creativity by making their recipes. And you can confidently go to their restaurants for an outstanding meal.

Godetevi! Enjoy!

Chapel Hill

Charlie Deal

Charlie Deal
at Jujube

Jujube
Glen Lennox Shopping Center
(next to Bin 54: Steak and Cellar)
1201-L Raleigh Rd. (N.C. 54 at U.S. 15/501)
Chapel Hill, N.C. 27514
919-960-0555
info@jujuberestaurant.com
www.jujuberestaurant.com

Directions
From Raleigh, take I-40 West to Exit 273A toward Chapel
Hill. Follow Raleigh Road (N.C. 54) through several lights
to Glen Lennox Shopping Center, on the right. Jujube is in
the strip mall next to Bin 54. From Durham, take I-40 East
to Exit 273. Turn toward Chapel Hill and follow Raleigh
Road to Glen Lennox Shopping Center, located just
before the U.S. 15/501 overpass. From Chapel Hill, follow
South Road (Raleigh Road) to the U.S. 15/501 overpass
and Glen Lennox Shopping Center, on the immediate left.

Cuisine
This chef-owned restaurant serves Asian fusion cuisine with
local ingredients.

The name of the restaurant Jujube is Chinese. Chef Charlie Deal says,
"It's the name of a Chinese date, the fruit of harmony. I was looking for a
name for the restaurant and thumbing through an encyclopedia of Asian
cooking and came across it and thought, 'Well, fruit of harmony isn't bad
for a name.'"

Jujube lives up to its name by serving Asian fusion food that wins
rave reviews. Visitors to the Glen Lennox strip mall in Chapel Hill don't
realize they have entered an outstanding restaurant until they see the
walls painted a rich persimmon color and a Key lime green. The effect is

Interior of Jujube

heightened if they go through a bamboo curtain and enter the outdoor patio landscaped in spring and summer with an abundance of flowers, shrubs, and grasses.

Jujube seats eighty-two inside and forty outside, including twelve at the long wooden bar. Though the cuisine is predominantly Asian fusion, guests can also enjoy Italian on Wednesdays. Charlie believes that the most important characteristic of his food is that it is authentic.

Charlie grew up in the San Francisco Bay area, always with good food at home because both his parents loved to cook. In school, he was a serious student who focused on science and math. But because his father encouraged him to take jobs, he washed dishes in restaurants when he was as young as fourteen and continued to work in restaurants through high school and college. He entered the University of California at Berkeley and majored in genetic engineering. But by that time, he had already become a "lifer" in the food industry, so he made the decision to follow his passion and become a cook.

After leaving college, he got his first major job at Oliveto Café and Restaurant in Oakland, where he worked under Chef Curt Clingman (now at Jojo's in Oakland). Clingman taught him the basics of "how to sear fish, braise beef, and make stock." The lessons were invaluable. In 1995, Charlie opened his own California restaurant, Oswald. In 1998, he opened his second, Charlie Hong Kong. "No one is self-taught," he says. "I was being taught by the world."

All the while, after work, he and his fellow restaurant workers went to Asian restaurants in San Francisco and San Jose, where Charlie learned through his palate the delicate cuisines of China, Vietnam, and other Asian countries. He would taste a good version of a dish and say, "Oh, that's how you do it."

And he learned from reading. "Books in the hands of someone who spends sixty hours a week in the kitchen can make an incredible impression," he says. His favorites were the books by Charmaine Solomon, a Sri Lankan who clearly "understood Asian food." Charlie especially referred to her *Encyclopedia of Asian Food*. Also, he used Madhur Jaffrey's *World of the East Vegetarian Cooking*.

Since he had already learned kitchen skills by the time he left Berkeley, and since he felt he had paid his dues by working for years at minimum wage, Charlie made the decision not to go to culinary school. Instead, he learned on the job, first at Oliveto and then at an Asian restaurant in Ketchum, Idaho, the Globus Noodle. He was there for only a few months before taking over the kitchen. Impressed, owner John Sweek took him on a tour of China for three weeks. His background in Asian cooking was thus set, preparing him for his upcoming adventure in North Carolina.

Charlie was on track to run and own restaurants when he met Diana, the woman who would become his wife. Because they wanted to own a house together and could not afford one in California, they began looking in other parts of the country. Through research and then visits, they ended up in the Triangle in 2002, buying a house in North Durham.

In a move that was to set Charlie's future, one of the first things the couple did when they arrived was to ask someone to recommend an upscale place for food and drink. They were referred to PariZade in Durham, and that was where Charlie's venture into Triangle restaurants began. That night at PariZade, sitting a few seats down from them was Giorgios Bakatsias, the owner. They struck up a conversation they continued at another of Giorgios's restaurants, Vin Rouge. That conversation lasted most of the night. Thanks to that meeting, Charlie joined Giorgios's group, which was opening several restaurants.

Charlie first opened the now-defunct Grasshopper, which was next door to Vin Rouge at the site where Blu Seafood and Bar now operates. Then the group wanted to open a steakhouse, now Bin 54: Steak and Cellar, along with an Asian restaurant. Charlie became 80 percent owner of Jujube. Giorgios still drops by every few months.

"Jujube's is authentic food inspired by the flavors of Asia, but not straight-up Asian," Charlie says. "I've had years of cooking, and I'm not going to forget that experience. It's important to be authentic. I live in central North Carolina and use food from here. I go to the Durham Farmers' Market on Saturday and the Carrboro Farmers' Market on Wednesday afternoons. Plus, farmers deliver to the restaurant."

When Charlie came to Durham, his ambition was to open a restaurant featuring his personal passion, Mexican food. Dos Perros is soon to open at 200 North Magnum Street in Durham. The name honors his two dogs at home. Dos Perros will be a "spatially upscale, traditional Mexican restaurant," Charlie says. "It is my favorite food in the whole world— profound, noble, and beautiful. Dos Perros will feature classic cuisine for dining and a *taqueria* in the bar."

Charlie says, "Every night, I have parties for a living. That's what I do. And that's part of what I love, giving dinner parties for about ten friends. And our cuisine at the restaurant is very simple. I like to think of our food as not too cerebral."

He offers a tasting menu but cautions those who ask for it to be sure the person they are with is equally into food. Otherwise, he counsels them to have a simple dinner and enjoy each other, as diners consistently do for lunch and dinner at Jujube.

Chef Charlie Deal's Recipes

CRAB AND SHRIMP CAKES WITH CORN AND GREEN CHILI CURRY
Serves 10

Crab and Shrimp Cakes
1 pound peeled and deveined shrimp, finely chopped
1 pound lump crab
1 cup cooked rice noodles, chopped into 1-inch lengths
1 bunch scallions, thinly sliced
½ bunch cilantro, chopped
½ stalk lemon grass, white part only, finely chopped
2 tablespoons fish sauce
3 tablespoons sweet chili sauce (available in groceries'
    Asian aisles)

½ cup mayonnaise
Breadcrumbs

Mix first 9 ingredients and chill for at least 1 hour. Form into 3-ounce balls and roll in breadcrumbs.

Corn and Green Chili Curry

4 ears corn, shucked, kernels cut from cob (2 cups
    frozen kernels may be substituted)
1 medium onion, diced
1 jalapeño, seeded and diced
2 tablespoons green curry paste, or to taste
2 13.5-ounce cans coconut milk
2 tablespoons fish sauce

Sauté corn, onions, and jalapeño briefly. Add curry paste and cook until aromatic. Add coconut milk and fish sauce and simmer at least 15 minutes.

To assemble, preheat oven to 400 degrees. Heat 1 tablespoon oil per crab cake in a nonstick pan. Add cakes, being careful not to crowd. Brown on 1 side and turn over. Place in oven for 10 minutes. Remove and serve on plates over corn and green chili curry.

LIME-COCONUT RICE PUDDING WITH BASIL-NECTARINE COMPOTE

Serves 4

Pudding

1 cup milk
3 cups coconut milk
½ cup sugar
⅓ cup jasmine rice, soaked in water for 30 minutes
Zest and juice of ½ lime

Heat milk, coconut milk, sugar, and rice until boiling. Simmer covered about 25 minutes until rice is soft. Remove from heat and stir in lime zest and juice. Flavor should be simple with a touch of lime. Ladle into serving bowls.

Basil-Nectarine Compote

½ cup water

Juice of ½ lime

¼ cup sugar

2 nectarines, pitted and cut into bite-sized pieces

¼ cup basil leaves, cut into thin strips

Heat water, lime juice, and sugar, bringing to a slow boil. Reduce to a thick syrup, being careful not to overcook. Toss with nectarines and basil.

Allow to rest for at least 15 minutes. Serve over pudding.

Alex Gallis
at Cypress on the Hill

Cypress on the Hill
308 West Franklin St.
Chapel Hill, N.C. 27516
919-537-8817
www.cypressonthehill.com
Directions
From Raleigh, take I-40 West to Exit 270. Turn left at the
light and follow U.S. 15/501 Business (Durham–Chapel
Hill Boulevard) to Chapel Hill. Take the Franklin Street
exit, to the right. Follow Franklin Street past Columbia
Street to West Franklin Street. Cypress on the Hill is on
the right. From Durham, take U.S. 15/501 Business to
Chapel Hill. Take the Franklin Street exit. Follow the
above directions to the restaurant. Parking is on the
premises.
Cuisine
This chef-owned restaurant serves New American
cuisine featuring fresh local ingredients whenever
possible.

Executive Chef Alex Gallis has lived in North Carolina since he was
six months old, first in Durham, then in Chapel Hill. He considers himself
a Chapel Hillian, so much so that when he stood on the front stoop of his
new restaurant and saw people walking on Franklin Street, tears came to
his eyes.

Alex Gallis

His earliest memories of food are linked to summers at Sunset Beach, when his father, a doctor, traded medical treatment to fishermen for shrimp and squid. His father made a Greek stuffed squid with raisins and pistachios. And Alex remembers how the Japanese doctor who accompanied his family on those trips made tempura. Unforgettable.

Alex has an artistic bent—and also an outdoors bent. He initially left Chapel Hill to pursue a dream far removed from the restaurant business—skiing. His college degree is in ski management, as a matter of fact. He flew around the world as a ski manufacturer's representative.

But as a husband and the father of a young child, he decided to settle down. At that point, he realized that "the only thing I know how to do is cook." So, at the age of twenty-nine, he went to Johnson & Wales University in Charleston, South Carolina, to study cooking. In nine months, he got a two-year degree in the accelerated program.

While at Johnson & Wales, Alex worked at Fish, a Charleston restaurant. There, he learned about the vast variety of seafood available, a lesson he used at the restaurants he has worked in since.

After graduation, Alex went to work at Acme Food and Beverage in Carrboro, where he was head chef. Thanks to his work, *Bon Appétit* named Acme one of the top fifty neighborhood restaurants in the country.

He left to work with Chef Ben Barker at Magnolia Grill, where he served as *chef de cuisine* for five years. "It was a great five years," Alex says. "I learned so much—about taking care of ingredients, ordering just what you need so things don't sit around, being careful about the end-of-the-week order."

And about cooking. "He made me a much better cook and helped me a lot in my food conceptualization," Alex says. "I learned about the way he cooks, the way he layers flavors. If there's bacon in the dish, then everything is cooked in bacon fat. Same thing with ham."

One of the influences Ben Barker had on Alex was his use of fresh local products. "Ben uses the freshest local ingredients, same as me. I owe a lot to Ben and Karen Barker for letting me work as *chef de cuisine* and for having trust in me to handle the kitchen when they were out of town," Alex says.

But there's a difference between them. "Ben's food is very rustic and straightforward," he says. "I'm a little more into artistic plating. I like clean, pretty plates. I guess that's my artistic background."

His menu is 50 percent Southern, in tribute to his mother's influence;

25 percent Greek, in tribute to his father and his family; and 25 percent Asian. "It's fine to focus on more than one type of cuisine. I enjoy all types of food. For example, I have a dish from the Austrian Alps, where I skied. It's a venison dish from humanely killed deer that I get from a ranch in Texas," he says. "It's more expensive, but everything is not about making money."

The name Cypress on the Hill comes from an experience on the Black River in Pender County, North Carolina, where he saw cypress trees growing wild in water with Spanish moss hanging from the branches. "They are the most majestic trees on the planet," Chef Alex says.

Interior of Cypress on the Hill

Executive Chef Alex Gallis's Recipes

PAN-SEARED BLACK SEA BASS WITH STEW OF WHITE BEANS, PANCETTA, WILD MUSHROOMS, AND GLAZED BEETS

Serves 4

Beets

1 medium red beet
1 medium golden beet
1 bunch chiogga beets (another colorful combination of 7 or 8
    small beets may be substituted)
Olive oil
Salt and pepper to taste
1 tablespoon butter
½ cup honey

Preheat oven to 400 degrees. Prepare beets to roast. Cut off stems and leaves and wash beets in cold water. Place beets in a roasting pan and drizzle with olive oil. Add salt and pepper. Cover pan tightly with foil and roast in oven for about 1 hour until beets are soft.

Remove beets from oven and cool to a comfortable temperature. Peel beets and dice them into ½-inch cubes. Heat butter in a sauté pan. Add beets to warm, then add honey to glaze. Set aside.

White Beans

1 pound dried white beans, soaked overnight in water
    and rinsed (canned beans may be substituted)
½ pound pancetta, diced small
Olive oil
1 cup Vidalia onion, diced small
1 tablespoon minced garlic
1 tablespoon fresh thyme
Chicken stock as needed
Salt and pepper to taste
1 sprig rosemary leaves

Cook beans in water to cover about 1 hour until tender.

Drain beans and rinse under cold water. In a large sauté pan over medium-high heat, render pancetta in olive oil until crispy. Add onions and sauté for 3 minutes. Add garlic and sauté 1 minute. Add beans and thyme, stirring to mix. Add chicken stock to cover. Bring to a boil, then reduce heat and simmer until beans are still tender but not falling apart. Season with salt and pepper and add rosemary for flavor after cooking is complete. Keep warm.

Wild Mushrooms

1 tablespoon butter
1 tablespoon olive oil
1 pound fresh wild mushrooms, finely minced

Heat butter and olive oil. Add mushrooms and sear over high heat for 3 to 4 minutes to caramelize.

Add mushrooms to white bean stew and heat through. Keep warm. Adjust salt and pepper as necessary.

Porcini Broth

½ cup dried porcini mushrooms
4 cups water
Salt and pepper to taste
2 sticks unsalted butter

Combine mushrooms and water in a stockpot. Bring to a boil, then reduce heat and simmer 30 minutes. Remove mushrooms and strain broth through a very fine sieve. Squeeze any liquid in cooled mushrooms into reserved broth. Finely chop mushrooms and return them to broth. Reserve mushrooms and broth, keeping warm. Add salt and pepper. Turn off heat. Whisk butter into warm broth and emulsify with an immersion blender.

Black Sea Bass

1 tablespoon peanut oil
4 8-ounce sea bass fillets
1 tablespoon butter

Preheat oven to 400 degrees. In a cast-iron skillet, heat

peanut oil over high heat. Add fillets skin side down and cook about 1 minute. Add butter, cook another minute, and flip. Move skillet to oven for about 3 minutes to finish cooking.

To serve, place white bean stew in a large bowl as a bed for fillets. Ladle broth around fillets and onto beans. Top fish with glazed beets.

Bret Jennings

Bret Jennings
at Elaine's on Franklin

Elaine's on Franklin
454 West Franklin St.
Chapel Hill, N.C. 27516
919-960-2770
info@elainesonfranklin.com
www.elainesonfranklin.com

Directions
From Raleigh, take I-40 West to Exit 270. Turn left at the light, follow U.S. 15/501 Business (Durham–Chapel Hill Boulevard) to Chapel Hill, and take the Franklin Street exit. Follow Franklin past Columbia Street. Elaine's is on the right. From Durham, follow U.S. 15/501 Business to Chapel Hill, take the Franklin Street exit, and follow the directions above. Valet parking is available.

Cuisine
This chef-owned restaurant serves world cuisine with local ingredients.

Chef Bret Jennings combines his experiences as traveler and diner with his conviction that local products create the best cuisine. From the day he opened his restaurant in 1999, he was one of the first to go local. He has maintained a "great relationship with farmers, local producers, fishmongers, and livestock breeders," he says.

Bret has packed an extraordinary number of experiences into an astonishingly short time, all of which has led to his "world cuisine made with local ingredients." His restaurant is the culmination of the culinary skills he learned through working with leading chefs and traveling extensively in Europe.

His story begins in Altavista, Virginia, where his family had lived for five or six generations. While his mother worked, he stayed with his grandmother, "an awesome cook," who made angel biscuits and country ham. "My favorite meal is breakfast," Bret says. His mother is also a cook. Her recipes have found their way into his current repertoire.

Bret attended North Carolina State University in Raleigh. When he got his degree in marketing in 1991, he expected to work in creative advertising. However, after fifty-five initial interviews but no callbacks for a second, he was depressed and took a job at Glenwood Grill in Raleigh. Eventually, he became chef there and discovered he enjoyed the work, which allowed him to be creative in combining textures and flavors.

"It was fun. I felt creative. The customers liked it," he says of his experience there. "Before, I was doing what other people were doing in cookbooks." He stayed at Glenwood Grill about four years.

Then a chance meeting with the *chef de cuisine* at Magnolia Grill in Durham led to his hiring at that restaurant. "It was at a completely different level there. Ben Barker is an excellent, excellent chef. Being there opened my eyes to the possibilities of many different techniques," Bret says. "Never having been to culinary school, I'd like to give credit to Ben for teaching so many cooks. It was hard work. Pressure. But I thrive off that pressure. It wasn't hard for me. And it was there I started to realize how well I could cook." He stayed at Magnolia Grill for about two years.

A "love interest" then interrupted that period of his life. Bret decided to follow her to Toulouse, France, where her parents had moved. But before leaving for Europe, he spent four months south of the border learning Mexican cuisine with friends from Glenwood Grill.

While in France, Bret worked in a couple of kitchens, visited vineyards, and ate at excellent restaurants. Through his visits to vineyards, he learned about *terroir*—how "the vines, the soil, the lay of the land affected the wine." He saw how regional everything was in France and "wanted to try it here." And he learned to "keep it simple."

In Europe, he also traveled to Italy, Spain, and the Czech Republic. "I speak pretty good Spanish, so I spent a long time in Spain," Bret says.

While in France, he made friends with the maître d' of Taillevent, a Michelin Three Star restaurant. Later, he would return to France for a *stage* (an apprenticeship) at the restaurant.

Back in the United States, he and his girlfriend settled in Washington, D.C., where he worked, upon the recommendation of Chef Ben Barker, at the three-hundred-seat Kinkead's restaurant. But coincidentally, a friend from Magnolia Grill was opening a restaurant in Chapel Hill, the Wild Turtle, and he lured Bret to the college town.

"It's very difficult for a die-hard N.C. State Wolfpack fan to live in Chapel Hill," Bret says.

He left the Wild Turtle shortly before it closed. "Ben Barker convinced me to go work for him again, this time as *sous chef*. Again, a fantastic kitchen, but I'd learned a lot and grown a lot. That time, I had more of a management role, which is pretty important," Bret says. Sharing an appreciation of good wine and good food, Ben and Bret continue to have a strong relationship.

When after two years he met the woman who would be his wife, Bret left Magnolia Grill for the second time, in this case to open his own restaurant. "This space came available. I got a couple of partners. And here we are," he says.

The restaurant's name, Elaine's on Franklin, came from the mother-in-law of one of the partners. She had just died after a battle with brain cancer. "It's a very positive tribute to her life," Bret says. "And it's kind of an elegant name. Doesn't imply bistro or trattoria or any other cuisine. It's a neutral name that allows me to cook ethnic food from Spain, Mexico, and the southeast states."

When he first opened his restaurant, "it was brilliant," Bret says. "There were no other white-tablecloth restaurants around. Now, there are ten at this end of Franklin, and we get along."

Two years after Bret opened Elaine's on Franklin, the nation experienced the tragedy of 9/11. But he had a *stage* scheduled at Taillevent in Paris and was not about to let anything stop him from going. To this day, recipes from Taillevent are on Bret's menu.

Bret does not use cookbooks. Instead, he refers to great meals he has had at outstanding restaurants such as Le Pastel in Toulouse, where the food, he says, is unbelievable; the French Laundry; Frontera Grill; and Mario's in Santa Fe. "I'll never forget these meals," Bret says. "I'm not a cookbook person. I read magazines for trends."

His cuisine includes all "my favorite things to eat," Bret says. His "well-thought-out world cuisine" is "traditional and respectful of the people the food comes from. I use my mother's recipes, my grandmother's, recipes from France, Mexico, the Czech Republic, Germany, chefs I've worked with. But mainly, my cuisine is from Mexico, France, my family, and Southern food."

Chef Bret likes his work. "We have a very nice chef community," he says. Now the father of three children, he works five days a week. "I'm not as much about money as about enjoying myself."

Chef Bret Jennings's Recipes

HUEVOS RANCHEROS
Serves 6

Black Beans
2 cups dried black beans
½ cup corn oil, divided
¼ yellow onion, diced
1 jalapeño, diced
1 clove garlic, minced
1 teaspoon cumin
2 quarts chicken stock
1 tablespoon salt

Soak black beans overnight.

In a large saucepot, add 2 to 3 tablespoons of the oil and fry onions and jalapeño over medium heat. Add garlic and cumin. Stir. Add beans and cover with chicken broth. Add salt and bring to a simmer. Cook gently, keeping beans covered with liquid, until just soft, about 1 hour depending on the beans. Strain in a colander, reserving liquid. Reheat saucepot, add remaining corn oil, and carefully add drained beans. Fry beans, stirring frequently. Add reserved liquid to thin slightly if necessary. Mash mixture gently with a potato masher. Check seasonings and set aside.

Beans can be made ahead and refrigerated for up to 2 days, which will improve the flavor.

Chorizo
½ pound chorizo
Corn oil

While beans are simmering, heat a sauté pan. Remove casing from chorizo and crumble onto a plate. In the pan over medium heat, add enough corn oil to cover bottom. Gently add chorizo, stirring until browned. Drain on paper towels and set aside in a warm place.

Salsa Verde

1 bunch cilantro, washed and coarsely chopped
1 clove garlic
¼ small red onion, sliced
1 tablespoon cumin
Salt to taste
Lime juice to taste
½ pound tomatillos, husked
3 jalapeños

While beans are simmering, put a pot of water on to boil. In a blender, add cilantro, garlic, onion, cumin, salt, and lime juice. When water boils, add tomatillos and jalapeños for 1 minute or until color starts to fade. Remove jalapeños and tomatillos with a slotted spoon and add to ingredients in blender. Carefully blend and check seasonings for taste. If necessary as you blend, moisten with some of the hot water.

Tortillas

3 6- to 8-inch tortillas
Corn oil
3 eggs
Radishes, sliced
Chili oil to taste
Queso cotija (a Mexican cheese similar to Parmesan)
Cilantro leaves

Heat a tortilla skillet or a cast-iron skillet, along with a nonstick skillet. In hot, dry tortilla skillet, warm tortillas. Hold in a clean, warm towel.

To assemble, spread warmed and mashed black beans on 2 of the tortillas and stack 1 on top of the other. Place third tortilla on top of the other 2. Coat the nonstick skillet with corn oil and add eggs. When done sunny side up, place eggs on top of the stack of refried beans and tortillas. Spoon salsa verde around the edges. Sprinkle chorizo on top of salsa verde. Sprinkle radishes and then chili oil around tortillas. Crumble cheese over and around tortillas. Sprinkle cilantro leaves in middle of dish. Cut into wedges to serve.

GREEN TOMATO–AVOCADO GAZPACHO
Serves 8

Gazpacho
6 poblano peppers
4 small green tomatoes or 9 tomatillos
½ small yellow onion
2 cloves garlic
3 cucumbers, peeled, seeded, and chopped
1 bunch cilantro with stems, washed
½ cup pumpkin seeds, toasted
Ground coriander to taste
Ground cumin to taste
Red wine vinegar to taste
Kosher salt to taste
Milk
1 avocado
Buttermilk

Roast peppers in a 500-degree oven until skins blister. Cool, then peel and seed. Divide first 11 ingredients in half and blend everything together in blender in 2 batches, adding just enough milk to help ingredients purée. Add avocado and blend just until emulsified. Pour into a chilling vessel, then thin gazpacho to desired thickness with buttermilk. Adjust salt, vinegar, and spices as necessary.

Garnish
¼ pound small shrimp, peeled and deveined
1 tablespoon tequila
1 red poblano pepper, roasted, seeded, peeled, and diced
Crispy corn tortilla strips
Red onion, thinly sliced
Pickled corn
Cilantro leaves

Chili oil
Lime juice

    Sear shrimp in a pan. Deglaze pan with tequila.
    Add shrimp and remaining ingredients as desired to tops of
bowls or serve on the side.

Interior of Elaine's on Franklin

Ed Kaminski

Ed Kaminski
at Bin 54: Steak and Cellar

Bin 54: Steak and Cellar
Glen Lennox Shopping Center
1201-M Raleigh Rd. (N.C. 54)
Chapel Hill, N.C. 27517
919-969-1155
www.bin54restaurant.com

Directions

From Raleigh, take I-40 West to Exit 273A. Follow
Raleigh Road (N.C. 54) toward Chapel Hill. Continue
through several lights to Glen Lennox Shopping Center,
on the right. Bin 54 is at the near end of the strip mall.
From Durham, take I-40 East to Exit 273. Turn toward
Chapel Hill on Raleigh Road and continue to Glen
Lennox Shopping Center, on the right just before the
U.S. 15/501 overpass. Bin 54 is at the near end of the
strip mall. From Chapel Hill, follow South Road (Raleigh
Road) to the U.S. 15/501 overpass and the shopping
center, on the left.

Cuisine

This restaurant serves prime steaks, fish, and braised
meats.

Though Executive Chef Ed Kaminski has been in North Carolina only
a short time, he has moved from grill chef to *sous chef* to *chef de cuisine* to
his current position of executive chef at Bin 54: Steak and Cellar. But that
is not surprising, considering how much he accomplished before arriving
in the state.

Ed's experience with his grandmother shaped his life to come. "She always had food going. One of the first things I made was apple pie. Grandma kept me cooking instead of doing whatever kids do. I was helping her roll out dough, shaping meatballs. I learned to love cooking, and when I ate what we made, I said, 'Holy cow, I did this.' Really, my grandma got me into this," he says.

His first job as a teen was with Chef Mark Spate at Ruga Restaurant in his home area, Oakland, New Jersey. He spent seven years there, working hard but loving the restaurant business. "I found it was what I wanted to do," Ed says.

After that, he went to the most important culinary school in North America, the Culinary Institute of America in Hyde Park, New York. While there, he had an externship with Chef Jean-Georges Vongerichten at his namesake restaurant in Manhattan, a four-star French fusion restaurant. "On my first day there, he handed me a big, giant black truffle worth about eight hundred bucks," says Ed.

He was not finished with schooling, though. His aim was to get a degree in hotel management at Fairleigh Dickinson University, but the school proved too expensive. He transferred his credits to New Jersey's Montclair State University, where he earned his bachelor's degree in history.

He followed his girlfriend to Chapel Hill and got a job at Giorgios Bakatsias's Bin 54, named after its location on N.C. 54 and its bins of wine. The wines as much as the steaks define the restaurant. "We have wonderful wine, from Bordeaux to small wineries with productions below two thousand bottles," says Ed. "Sometimes, only four or five bottles are available, and we get three or four of those."

Ed describes himself as a perfectionist chef. "I look for consistency. I push for that really hard," he says. That attitude is important at a small fine-dining restaurant where he searches every day for the best products. The beef is cooked over 100 percent hickory. "We don't mask or hide the natural flavors. We buy top-notch ingredients, prime and Black Angus beef, and that's how we present it. Giorgios says that 'we serve them naked.' "

Ed's philosophy of food and dining at Bin 54 includes the ambience. "We give the very best food, made simply. The restaurant brings everyone together in an elegant setting," he says. The restaurant's corporate dining rooms are frequently filled.

Working in the Giorgios Bakatsias group is rewarding. Other excellent chefs in the group, such as Chef Matthew Kelly from Vin Rouge in Durham, come to Bin 54. "We bounce ideas off one another," says Chef Ed.

The high-end Bin 54 is located at the end of a strip mall, right next door to Jujube. But once customers enter, they are in another world.

Executive Chef Ed Kaminski's Recipes

BRAISED SHORT RIBS

Serves 2 to 3

Salt and pepper to taste
1 pound short ribs (10 per pound)
Vegetable oil
¼ cup chopped carrots
¼ cup chopped celery
½ cup chopped onions
½ cup plus 2 tablespoons red wine
¼ cup tomato paste
3 cups good-quality beef stock
2 bay leaves
2 sprigs thyme

Preheat oven to 350 degrees. Salt and pepper ribs and set aside. In a large ovenproof braising pan or a Dutch oven, heat oil over medium-high heat. Brown ribs on all sides. Remove ribs and excess fat in bottom of pan, leaving about 2 tablespoons. Caramelize vegetables in pan. Add wine to pan and deglaze. Add tomato paste, beef stock, bay leaves, and thyme. Bring to a simmer. Return ribs to pan, cover, and place in oven for about 3 hours until fork tender.

Remove ribs, degrease the sauce, and simmer if necessary until correct consistency is reached. Adjust consistency of sauce by adding beef stock or cooking to thicken. Remove bay leaves and thyme stems. Season to taste.

ED KAMINSKI ON HOW TO COOK A STEAK

"Choose a high-quality piece of meat with good marbling and bright red color. I recommend certified Angus beef prime

Interior of Bin 54: Steak and Cellar

cuts. Figure on half a pound to 1 pound per serving. Pat the steak dry and season with kosher salt and freshly ground black pepper. I recommend it 'naked,' seasoned only with salt and pepper, so as not to mask the natural flavor of a good cut of meat. But if you choose to add other herbs and spices, make sure they are of the highest available quality and use them sparingly.

"Prepare the grill. If your grill allows you to add wood chips, soak them in water first and experiment with different varieties. I recommend hickory. Heat the grill and cook over medium to medium-high heat. Place the meat directly on the grill without cooking spray or oil. The most important rule of grilling a great steak is to allow it to develop a nice seared flavor. I recommend taking a hands-off approach to letting it cook. If you move it too much initially, it will stick to the grill.

"Cook approximately 5 minutes per side per 1-inch thickness for medium-rare. Turn the steak 45 degrees for classic 'diamond' markings.

"When the steak is cooked to your desired doneness, let the meat rest. This allows the steak's natural juices to be reincorporated into the meat. My general rule is to let the steak rest for a quarter of its cooking time. For example, if it cooked for 20 minutes, let it rest for at least 5 minutes.

"To serve, cut the steak into quarter-inch slices by cutting against the grain of the meat."

James Reale

James Reale
at *Carolina Crossroads*
(*Carolina Inn*)

Carolina Crossroads in the Carolina Inn

211 Pittsboro St.
Chapel Hill, N.C. 27516
800-962-8519 or 919-933-2001
www.carolinainn.com

Directions

From Raleigh, take I-40 West to Exit 270. Turn left and
follow U.S. 15/501 Business (Durham–Chapel Hill
Boulevard), staying on the right for several blocks. At
the Franklin Street exit, veer right and follow Franklin
Street for several blocks to South Columbia Street.
Turn left and go one block to West Cameron Avenue.
Turn right, then immediately left onto Pittsboro Street.
Turn into the parking lot. From Durham, take U.S.
15/501 Business toward Chapel Hill and follow the
directions above.

Cuisine

This AAA Four Diamond and Mobile Four Star
restaurant in the Carolina Inn serves New American
cuisine with Italian overtones, using local produce.

Executive Chef James Reale at the Carolina Inn in Chapel Hill is a
perfect match for the hotel's warmth and welcoming spirit. Known as
"Chef Jimmy" to all who come in contact with him, he was born in the
Bronx. In 1976, at the age of three, he moved to Fayetteville with his
parents to be with their extended Italian and Lebanese family. This family
and its kitchen get-togethers formed the basis of Jimmy's love of food and
his unique cuisine.

"The kitchen was the gathering point. Every time we got together, it was based around the kitchen and wine. There was a lot of cooking going on and a crowd of people, including all the cousins," says Jimmy.

He stayed with his family until he graduated from high school, when he went to Greenville. He tentatively planned on going to East Carolina University, but finances got in the way. To support himself, Jimmy got a job in the only field he knew something about. His grandfather owned a wine and beer distributorship, and he had helped with that business in high school. So he got a job in a pizza parlor in Greenville.

"That was all I knew," Jimmy says. "And from then on, I cooked. Once I was doing it and making money, I said that I could do this as a profession. I fell in love with cooking. After all, I'd grown up cooking with my mom all the traditional Italian and Lebanese dishes."

Though he investigated other culinary schools, he decided on Johnson & Wales University in Charleston, South Carolina. He liked the city well enough to spend the next few years there. His externship—usually taken with a practicing chef while still in school—was with a buddy who had graduated from Johnson & Wales and opened his own restaurant. Coincidentally, Jimmy did a one-day *stage*, or apprenticeship, at the Carolina Inn in the banquet department.

After graduation from Johnson & Wales, Jimmy worked at a restaurant in Raleigh for about six months before the Carolina Inn hired him in 1999. In 2000, he quickly moved to the Paul J. Rizzo Conference Center, which like the Carolina Inn is owned by the University of North Carolina at Chapel Hill. He stayed there as executive chef for six and a half years before being selected from more than two hundred applicants for the position of executive chef of the Carolina Inn. The hotel's restaurant, Carolina Crossroads, boasts Mobil Four Star and AAA Four Diamond ratings.

"Stepping into the inn was like a whole new world. The restaurant end of it puts out great food. There's the banquet end, and now I oversee all the food," says Jimmy. Though he has thirty-eight cooks working for him, and though the hotel annually does about $7.5 million of business in food, he "actually does some of the cooking. I'm a hands-on chef."

The most important of the cooks working for him are *Chef de Cuisine* Jeremy Blankenship, who formerly worked under Chef Ben Barker at Magnolia Grill, and the pastry chef, Suzanne Menius. Together, Jimmy and Jeremy work on the menus, choosing the dishes. "I love writing menus. I'd rather be in the kitchen than at a desk," says Jimmy. All the

Interior of Carolina Crossroads

banquet menus are now Jimmy's, and he has converted the restaurant menus to his style of dishes.

Jimmy's food is influenced by his upbringing. "I tend to go back to how I grew up eating with Italian and Lebanese flavors," he says. "For example, braciole. It's Mom's dish, and now it's on the tasting menu. I make it with beef, prosciutto, caramelized onion rings, locatelli. Tie it up, braise it in tomato sauce. When ready to serve, I slice across, so you get rings of the dish. I serve it with fried green tomatoes for the Southern influence." For a real Southern dish, he serves chicken pot pie "with baked biscuits on top."

The truth is, he "likes cooking all kinds of things. I love Spanish. I'm making fish tacos. I love Asian. I get a great response from the customers," he says.

One day in the kitchen, a cook diffidently sliced a piece of bread horizontally. He questioned Jimmy, who took the bread and knife from the young man and demonstrated how to do it, cutting the two whole pieces into four as an answer. "I'm not a yeller. I want things done the correct way, but I'm really laid-back."

Like many chefs throughout the country, Jimmy not only uses local products, he features them on his menus. "I go to the farmers' market every Wednesday and Saturday and get whatever is beautiful out there. I'll serve tomatoes fresh from the farmers' market with Chapel Hill Creamery farmers' cheese and a dressing of fig balsamic reduction," he says. "Vegetables come in fresh every day. What's fresh, what's local. I'd rather go to the farmers' market and pick out beautiful things."

Chef Jimmy is a natural cook. "I enjoy what I do. It's gratifying to walk through the restaurant and have people tell you how good it is," he says. "I get happy when people enjoy what I cooked."

Executive Chef James Reale's Recipes

FARMERS' MARKET TOMATO SOUP WITH ARUGULA PESTO CROSTINI

Yields 4 to 6 appetizer portions

Tomato Soup
6 vine-ripened tomatoes (use fresh tomatoes from a farmers'
    market, if available)
1 yellow onion, roughly chopped
1 large carrot, roughly chopped
1 cup celery, roughly chopped
Vegetable oil
2 cloves garlic, chopped
1 to 2 cups vegetable stock
¼ cup half-and-half
Salt and pepper to taste
Dark balsamic vinegar to taste
Chopped fresh herbs such as basil, parsley, and oregano

Peel, slice, and roughly chop tomatoes. Once cut, tomatoes should measure out to roughly 3 cups. In a large pot over medium heat, sauté onions, carrots, and celery in a little oil until vegetables start to soften. Add garlic and cook for 1 minute. Add tomatoes. Add vegetable stock to cover vegetables. Bring to a simmer and cook for 30 minutes. Add half-and-half. Remove from heat and purée in blender or with an immersion blender. Add salt, pepper, and balsamic vinegar. Serve in bowls garnished with fresh herbs.

Arugula Pesto Crostini

¼ cup pine nuts
¼ cup walnuts
1 cup arugula, loosely packed
1 cup basil, leaves only, loosely packed
½ cup grated locatelli or other hard Italian cheese
1 clove garlic
2 tablespoons extra-virgin olive oil
Salt and pepper to taste
1 small baguette

Toast pine nuts by placing them in a dry skillet over medium-low heat. Shake skillet frequently to ensure even browning; nuts will burn quickly if not watched carefully. Toast walnuts by baking on a cookie sheet in a 300-degree oven for 10 to 15 minutes until golden. Chop walnuts. Place pine nuts, walnuts, and next 6 ingredients in a food processor and purée into a thick pesto. Slice baguette, drizzle with additional olive oil, and toast under broiler. Spread pesto on toasted baguette. Serve with Farmers' Market Tomato Soup.

FRISEE GREENS, CHICKEN, GRILLED PEAR, CARAMELIZED ONIONS, TOASTED PECANS, AND GOAT CHEESE SALAD WITH SHERRY DRESSING

Serves 1 to 4

Sherry Dressing

Makes about 2 cups
½ cup aged sherry vinegar
1 teaspoon roasted garlic
1 shallot, sliced
¼ cup honey
½ teaspoon Dijon mustard
Salt and pepper to taste
1½ cups grape seed oil or similar oil

Combine all ingredients in a blender and blend for 30

seconds. Adjust seasonings as needed and set aside. This dressing can be kept in the refrigerator for up to 2 weeks.

Salad

1½ cups frisee greens
Salt and pepper to taste
3 ounces grilled chicken breast
Vegetable oil
1 Bosc pear, peeled, cored, and quartered
1 medium Vidalia onion, peeled and julienned
1 tablespoon pecans, plus extra for plate
1 tablespoon goat cheese, crumbled, plus extra for plate

Rinse greens, then remove as much water from them as possible. Cut greens a couple of times with a knife. Salt and pepper chicken. Lightly oil it. Grill chicken, let cool, then cut into 4 strips. Grill pear on all sides for about 5 minutes. Sauté onions in pan over medium heat for about 15 minutes until sugars caramelize and onions are brown. Toast pecans by placing them on a cookie sheet in a 300-degree oven for 10 to 15 minutes.

To assemble, place greens, pecans, goat cheese, ⅛ cup sherry dressing, and a pinch of salt and pepper in a mixing bowl. Mix well. Place mixture in the middle of a large plate or 4 small plates. Place chicken around salad mix. Scatter onions on top of chicken. Slice quartered pears into fans; do not cut all the way through, so pears will fan out. Place on top of salad mix. Place extra goat cheese and pecans and a little dressing around the plate.

Adam Rose
at Il Palio (Siena Hotel)

Il Palio in the Siena Hotel
1505 East Franklin St.
Chapel Hill, N.C. 27514
800-223-7379 or 919-929-4000
www.sienahotel.com/ilpalio.cfm

Directions
> From Raleigh, take I-40 West to Exit 270. Turn left toward
> Chapel Hill on U.S. 15/501 Business (Durham–Chapel
> Hill Boulevard) and continue to the Franklin Street exit, to
> the right. Go ¾ mile to the hotel, located on the right just
> before the third Franklin Street light. From Durham, follow
> U.S. 15/501 Business toward Chapel Hill to the Franklin
> Street exit. Follow the directions above.

Cuisine
> This AAA Four Star restaurant in the Siena Hotel serves
> classic Italian cuisine using fresh local ingredients.

Executive Chef Adam Rose credits his team of approximately twenty-one "talented and passionate cooks" and kitchen workers whom he "counts on day after day" for Il Palio's remarkable classic Italian cuisine. Il Palio is named for the annual Tuscany bareback horserace through the streets of Siena, the city that gave the hotel its name.

Adam received his training at the Culinary Institute of America. He attended not because he wanted to be a chef but because he thought the training would make him a better manager. He had grown up in a family

Adam Rose

of hotel and restaurant managers. His grandfather was a restaurateur and chef. His great-grandparents owned hotels in the Catskill Mountains of New York, and he often heard his mother tell stories of spending summers there and winters in Miami Beach. Ironically, he fell in love with cooking at the Culinary Institute of America. Since that time in the late 1990s, "I realized I really wanted to be in the kitchen," he says.

From 2001 to 2004, he operated his own restaurant with a partner. That restaurant, Soma, served casual cuisine. Adam acted as chef. When the restaurant closed, he realized he needed the experience of working with top chefs in fine-dining establishments.

The first chef he worked with in New York City was John Lindenauer, now the *chef de cuisine* for *Bon Appétit*; Lindenauer's background included work with world-famous chef Jean-Georges Vongerichten. Adam then worked with Chef Tom Colicchio, owner of the Craft restaurants and former owner of Gramercy Tavern, and Chef Tim Oltmans, owner of Jack the Horse Tavern in Brooklyn.

Adam came to North Carolina in 2006 primarily because it was the kind of place he and his wife, Hailey, a sommelier, wanted to raise their little girl. Their 650-square-foot apartment in New York would not do. The two heard that North Carolina had a great food culture and that people were moving to the state. "Everything I heard about the area is true. Great food community, great place to raise a child. Life has been good to me lately," Adam says.

They came expecting that openings in Wilson and Tarboro would lead to work, but those opportunities fell through. By the time Hailey became sommelier at Il Palio, Adam took temporary work with two local chefs—Charlie Deal of Jujube and Bret Jennings of Elaine's on Franklin. Adam served as pastry chef at Jujube and worked nights cooking and expediting the line at Elaine's. Both Charlie Deal and Bret Jennings knew Adam was looking for an executive chef position.

Hailey arranged for Adam's interview for the position at Il Palio, but Adam had to prove himself by cooking for the hotel owners for two straight days. They apparently loved what they sampled, since Adam is now executive chef at Il Palio. Their choice was a good one. Recently, the restaurant received its highest ranking from AAA since the hotel opened.

"I have a passion for what I do. Otherwise, I couldn't do it six days a week. There are so many easier ways to earn a living than being in a restaurant," says Adam. "But I've got the greatest job in the world. There are exceptional moments like cooking live at the Flight for Hope event." Flight for Hope keeps one jet and five pilots on standby at all times for flights east of the Mississippi River to facilitate organ donations for children.

Under Adam's direction, the cuisine at Il Palio is classical Italian cooked by an American. "The cuisine of Italy as a whole is so remarkable," says Adam. "Now, I judge every restaurant I go to on its Bolognese sauce." At Il Palio, he says, "there's great food, some of the best ingredients that we can buy. I love what I'm doing. I get to work with local farmers like Eliza MacLean of Cane Creek Farm, who raises heritage pork, and Bill Dow of Ayrshire, who has produce. The farmers are neat, passionate people, hard workers. There's nothing better than a summer tomato. You don't have to do anything to it. A little olive oil, salt, and pepper. Makes the job easy."

Adam's philosophy of food and cooking is to keep it simple. "Make the food tasty with strong, bold flavors. Don't crowd plates. Local is better. Don't put anything on the plate that you can't eat," he says. "I like great service, and we have training on that every day. But I'm in the business of feeding people. Service doesn't have to be pretentious." The restaurant serves three meals a day.

He is a perfectionist, like many great chefs. "To truly do the job," Chef Adam says, "you can't not be a perfectionist. I sign my name to every plate. I want every plate to be as great as the previous one. That doesn't happen by accident. It takes a lot of work, a lot of dedication to details. It takes a crew of people I can trust. I have chefs that help me run this kitchen, and they have to understand the philosophy. I lead from the front and show what I want. We're not going to serve substandard food."

Executive Chef Adam Rose's Recipes

Tomato Bisque
Serves 6 to 8

2 28-ounce cans whole tomatoes in juice
¾ cup brown sugar
4 shallots, finely chopped
1 stick unsalted butter
6-ounce can tomato paste
½ cup all-purpose flour

Interior of Il Palio

1½ cups chicken stock
½ cup heavy cream
Cayenne to taste (start with ¼ teaspoon)
Allspice to taste (start with ¼ teaspoon)
Salt and pepper to taste (start with ¼ teaspoon each)

Preheat oven to 350 degrees. With clean hands, squeeze juice out of tomatoes. Reserve juice. Combine brown sugar and tomatoes in a roasting pan and bake about 45 minutes until dry.

In a soup pot, sauté shallots in butter until soft. Add tomato paste and combine evenly. Stir in flour evenly and cook for 2 to 3 minutes, stirring often. Add juice from tomatoes and chicken stock. Simmer for 45 minutes to 1 hour.

Stir in baked tomatoes and cream. Allow to cool slightly before puréeing in a blender or a food processor, or purée immediately with an immersion blender. Add cayenne and allspice, stir, and simmer for 30 to 40 minutes. Season with salt and pepper.

Serve with melted cheese crostini of your choice.

CHOCOLATE-ESPRESSO CUSTARD

Serves 7 to 9

1½ cups heavy cream
1½ cups half-and-half
7 tablespoons granulated sugar
¼ cup plus 1 tablespoon espresso beans
6 ounces bittersweet chocolate
¾ ounce unsweetened chocolate
9 egg yolks
1 tablespoon cognac
Fresh whipped cream
Chocolate shavings

Preheat oven to 325 degrees. In a heavy-bottomed saucepan, warm cream, half-and-half, sugar, and espresso beans over medium heat. Do not boil. Remove from burner and steep for 45 minutes or longer for more espresso flavor.

Meanwhile, melt the 2 chocolates in a double boiler, whisking until smooth and glossy. In a bowl, whisk yolks lightly. Rewarm cream. Strain cream with espresso beans through a fine strainer into melted chocolate and whisk together. Slowly, in a thin stream, add warmed cream mixture to yolks, whisking continuously. Add cognac. Whisk. Pour mixture ¾ way up medium-sized ramekins. Place in a pan filled with water halfway up ramekins. Cook about 45 minutes. Check for doneness; should jiggle slightly when shaken. Garnish with fresh whipped cream and chocolate shavings.

Bill Smith
at Crook's Corner

Crook's Corner
610 West Franklin St.
Chapel Hill, N.C. 27516
919-929-7643
www.crookscorner.com
Directions
> From Raleigh, take I-40 West to Exit 270. Turn
> left toward Chapel Hill on U.S. 15/501 Business
> (Durham–Chapel Hill Boulevard) and continue to
> the Franklin Street exit, to the right. Follow Franklin
> Street past Columbia Street to West Franklin Street.
> Crook's Corner is on the right. From Durham, follow
> U.S. 15/501 Business toward Chapel Hill, take the
> Franklin Street exit, and follow the directions above.

Cuisine
> This restaurant serves Southern cuisine featuring fresh
> seasonal ingredients.

The building has hubcaps on an outside wall and a pig on the roof, and Chef Bill Smith has an acclaimed cookbook, so you know your experience at Crook's Corner is going to be both unusual and yummy.

"I try to make food that's really good but not talked about all night. I find that really tedious," says Bill. "My goal for Crook's Corner is that people come here and enjoy themselves."

Bill Smith

Bill's first experiences with food were at home in New Bern. "I'm old enough that I came from a generation where people sat down to big family dinners," says Bill. "My most formative experiences were at my great-grandmother's lunch table. Every day except Sunday, there was a big sit-down meal. Napkins, china. Fabulous cook. An aunt would cook Sunday meals, and we'd get up stupefied."

Bill, an accomplished writer with an interest in music, co-founded Cat's Cradle, a live music venue in Carrboro. He entered the world of professional cooking gradually. He came to Chapel Hill to go to school during "hippie time," he says. He lived in big houses with several roommates, and they cooked elaborate meals—"nothing shabby," Bill says. A waitress at La Résidence told him the restaurant needed a potato peeler in the kitchen, and he took the job. When he came back from one of his trips to Europe, he got the same job again.

"What I liked about restaurant work was its flexibility," he says. "It must have taken, because I didn't set out to become a professional cook."

At La Résidence, Bill worked alongside the late Chef Bill Neal, who went through Julia Child's cookbooks recipe by recipe. Bill Smith gained a foundation in the French style of cooking and something more. "Bill Neal had a sense of adventurousness, an anything-goes attitude," says Bill Smith. "That came in very handy to me."

When La Résidence changed hands in 1992, the new owners, Tom and Frances Gualtieri, wanted a family-run restaurant. So Bill was no longer chef there. He went to Europe again at that time. Meanwhile, Gene Hamer, who owns Crook's Corner, had not found a replacement for the late Bill Neal. In 1993, Bill Smith told Hamer he would fill in. "But I'm not going to be in charge of anything," he said to Hamer. Looking back today, he adds, "Look what happens."

The purveyors who provide Crook's Corner with fresh produce and meats have been working with Bill for years, some since his La Résidence days. In addition to the usual, they bring in special crops—persimmons, heirloom pigs, the bounty of the region. Bill also frequents the Carrboro Farmers' Market and the Mexican stores, where he finds mangoes in season.

In the spring, he makes corned hams, a recipe unique to eastern North Carolina, he says. In the fall, he makes mango salad—"a recipe I swiped from Mexico." Both recipes are in his cookbook.

Recently, he made cakes using Nancie McDermott's *Southern Cakes*.

"I've never been much of a cake maker, but I worked my way through her book. I'm going to do it again, especially Lane Cake."

But it would be a mistake to think of Crook's Corner as simply a place to get down-home Southern cooking. Bill Smith has not forgotten Bill Neal's sense of adventure. "I inherited a repertoire that's very sound, and a whole lot comes from my growing up," says Bill of his ideas for his food. Recently, he wanted to make butterscotch pudding and could not find good butterscotch flavoring, so he tinkered until he found a perfect combination of molasses and vanilla to get his butterscotch.

Not just the food is memorable at Crook's Corner. Guests cherish the entire experience of being in a place where "everybody knows who you are if you come here often," says Bill. The wait staff tends to be older than most. "Half are people who have other interests," he says. "Artists, writers, musicians. The basic staff has been around as long as I have." His workers often go on to other restaurants. "I have people in half the restaurants in town," says Bill.

"Gene Hamer takes care of all the business stuff, the upkeep of the building," says Bill. "He's host at Sunday brunches, called 'The Drawing Room of Chapel Hill.' "

Interior of Crook's Corner

What Bill really wants is time to read. "I'm over sixty. Some days, I work from eight-thirty in the morning to midnight. Can't do that anymore, so I don't work all three weekend nights," he says. Still, he often mingles with guests at the restaurant and intends for his smiling face to be seen there for years to come.

Chef Bill's blog may be found at www.seasonedinthesouth.com/blog. He is the author of the 2005 cookbook, *Seasoned in the South: Recipes from Crook's Corner and from Home*, published by Algonquin Press of Chapel Hill. He was a semifinalist for the 2009 James Beard Award for Best Chef in the Southeast.

Chef Bill Smith's Recipes

BAKED WINTER SQUASH SOUP

Serves 8 to 10

2 medium-sized winter squash (any winter squash will do)
½ teaspoon salt
¼ teaspoon hot curry powder
½ tablespoon mild curry powder
2 tablespoons brown sugar
2 tablespoons butter
6 cloves garlic, peeled
4 cups heavy cream
Toasted pumpkin seeds for garnish

Preheat oven to 400 degrees. Wash squash well, then split lengthwise and scoop out seeds. (You may find microwaving squash for 4 to 5 minutes helps soften it for cutting.) Sprinkle cut sides with salt. Place squash cut sides up in a roasting pan. Divide the curry powders and brown sugar among the seed cavities, then top each with ½ tablespoon of the butter. Add garlic cloves to bottom of roasting pan. Cover tightly with a lid or foil and bake for 1 to 1½ hours until squash is thoroughly cooked and garlic cloves are very soft. Cooking time will vary according to type and size of squash.

When squash is done, remove from oven and allow to cool enough to handle, then scoop flesh from skins. Purée flesh along with garlic and any juice that has collected in seed cavities. You may purée the soup with a food mill, a food processor, or an immersion blender. Strain soup to remove unprocessed fiber. If any juice is left in pan, and if it tastes good, add it to puréed soup. Thin to a soup consistency with cream. The amount needed will vary according to moisture content of squash.

Reheat soup carefully, as it is easy to scorch. Taste for seasonings and add salt as needed. Serve topped with pumpkin seeds.

BUTTERSCOTCH PUDDING

Yields 8 to 10 ¾-cup servings

4 egg yolks
⅔ cup cornstarch
1 cup light brown sugar
1 cup granulated sugar
1 teaspoon salt
4 cups cold milk
2 cups half-and-half
1 tablespoon molasses
6 tablespoons cold butter, cut into 6 chunks
2 teaspoons vanilla

Beat yolks well with a whisk in a large mixing bowl and set aside. Put cornstarch, sugars, and salt in a large saucepan and whisk together as best you can. The brown sugar will probably be moist and will resist breaking up. Whisk 1 cup of the milk into sugar mixture and stir until more or less smooth. Then stir in the rest of the milk and the half-and-half. Put pan on medium heat and stir constantly until pudding begins to thicken. This will take 8 to 10 minutes. You can turn up the heat, but be careful of scorching. When pudding begins to thicken, very gradually pour a couple of cups of pudding mixture into yolks and whisk rapidly. Turn egg mixture back into saucepan. Simmer and stir until pudding is very thick; stir constantly to prevent clumping and scorching. Don't let mixture boil. Remove from heat, then whisk in molasses, butter, and vanilla.

This is delicious hot, but you really ought to let it set up. You may do this in a large bowl or in individual cups. One good option is to serve pudding with fresh whipped cream. A small amount of butterscotch extract will bump up flavor of pudding. Try adding ½ teaspoon at a time after turning egg mixture back into saucepan. Be careful not to add too much.

APPLE RUM CAKE

Chef Bill says, "This cake is easy, although the first time you make it, the technique may seem peculiar."

Serves 8 to 10

¾ cup dark rum
½ cup golden raisins
1 cup stale breadcrumbs
4 cups cooking apples, peeled, cored, thinly sliced, and
    sprinkled with a little lemon juice
Zest and juice of 1 orange
1½ teaspoons cinnamon
½ teaspoon vanilla
4 large eggs, separated
¾ cup sugar, divided
2 tablespoons unsalted butter
Pinch of salt
1 cup red currant jelly

Preheat oven to 375 degrees. Warm rum in a small saucepan on the stove, then steep raisins in it for 15 minutes to plump them. Put breadcrumbs in a large mixing bowl. Stir in rum and raisins, then fold in apples, orange zest, cinnamon, and vanilla. The mixture will be lumpy. Beat egg yolks with ½ cup of the sugar until pale and creamy. Fold into apple-breadcrumb mixture. This will be very thick.

Put a large cast-iron skillet on stove on the lowest possible heat. Add butter to melt. Swirl it around to coat skillet. Beat egg whites with salt and the rest of the sugar until shiny and firm, then fold into apple-breadcrumb mixture in thirds. Turn skillet heat up to high. When butter begins to sizzle, pour in the cake batter and even it out with a spatula. Allow cake to fry for 1 or 2 minutes. The butter will begin to come up around the sides of the batter and perhaps up through the middle as well.

Cover skillet with foil or a tight-fitting lid and place in oven. Bake for 25 to 30 minutes until cake begins to feel firm at center. If any batter sticks to your finger when you test it, it isn't quite ready. When cake is ready, remove lid and cook until top is brown and cake begins to pull away from sides of skillet. This will take at least 10 minutes, more in some ovens.

Remove skillet from oven and allow it to rest on a cake rack for 20 minutes. While cake is still warm, wobble skillet from side to side gently until cake dislodges and isn't sticking. Do this deliberately and gently. Place a cake plate over cake and flip skillet over; since the cast iron is heavy, you will need to follow through once you start. Sometimes, hot butter or sugar will drip out and startle you, but it won't be hot enough to hurt you. Pull skillet straight up and away. You should be looking at a beautiful cake.

Melt currant jelly in a small saucepan. Add enough orange juice to make it a little runny. While cake is still warm, pour jelly mixture through a sieve over cake to coat it. Some of the glaze will spread out around cake on plate.

This cake is good warm or cold but is particularly delicious warm with fresh whipped cream or vanilla ice cream. It reheats well in the microwave.

Chip Smith
at *Bonne Soirée*

Bonne Soirée
The Courtyard, No. 10
431 West Franklin St.
Chapel Hill, N.C. 27516
919-928-8388

Directions
From Raleigh, take I-40 West to Exit 270. Turn
left toward Chapel Hill on U.S. 15/501 Business
(Durham–Chapel Hill Boulevard) and continue to
the Franklin Street exit, to the right. Follow Franklin
Street past Columbia Street to West Franklin Street. The
Courtyard is on the left. Turn left on Robertson Street,
then make an immediate left into the parking lot. Enter
The Courtyard from the back. From Durham, take U.S.
15/501 Business toward Chapel Hill to the Franklin
Street exit and follow the directions above.

Cuisine
This chef-owned restaurant serves French cuisine with
Southern ingredients.

Chef Chip Smith is in exactly the place he wants to be—cooking at his little restaurant, Bonne Soirée. And that means that his wife and partner, Tina Vaughn, is there with him. In fact, Bonne Soirée would not be as special as it is without either of them.

Chip is the cook. "I cook 95 percent of the meals, and I think that's pretty cool. I like to prep, I like to cook, I like to clean. That's what I do," he says. He comes in early to make desserts and bake bread. Chip and Tina do not serve what they cannot make in-house.

Like the restaurant—which seats thirty-five and has eleven

Chip Smith

tables—the kitchen is small. Although Bonne Soirée is small, its reputation is huge because of Chip's cooking. He discovered that he loved working in a kitchen and cooking when he had a summer job at a Hilton Head restaurant. He ended up staying two years. He developed his cooking style in the years of his training, which began with a degree from the Culinary Institute of America. For his externship, he was lucky to land a place with Larry Forgione at American Place in New York City shortly after the restaurant had earned three stars from the *New York Times*. At the time, Forgione, who was celebrating an anniversary, invited guest chefs such as Mark Miller, Alice Waters, Wolfgang Puck, and Sheila Lukens to come to the restaurant on weekends. "It was a very exciting time. It set me on fire," says Chip.

"Larry was pretty much the Alice Waters of the East Coast. Cook with the seasons. Use what is available. Simple and of the area. Larry was a great first step into that," Chip says. "And that's what I mean when I say we're a French restaurant. He had figured out what made French cooking good."

He met Tina there on her first day. Coincidentally, that was also Chip's last day as an extern, though he came back to work weekends.

By the time he left Larry Forgione's American Place, he and Tina were a couple. They next went to work with Jean-Louis Palladin of the Watergate Hotel in Washington, D.C. "Jean-Louis was the best cook I worked with," says Chip. "What I learned there is the way I cook here."

From there, they went to The Inn at Little Washington in Washington, Virginia, where they spent two and a half years absorbing from Patrick O'Connell and Reinhardt Lynch the ways to please customers and cook. "There, I learned that a restaurant's success isn't just about food, but about everything—from the choice of toilet paper to the way the food is served."

When they left The Inn at Little Washington, they opened a restaurant called Carolina Blue in Kitty Hawk. While they were on the coast, the James Beard Foundation nominated Chip as one of the Southeast's best chefs.

Meanwhile, they explored. Every year in the down season, they spent a month in Paris, living on twenty dollars a day. And every chance they got, they came to the Triangle for wine tastings. In the end, they did not stay in Kitty Hawk because money was tight and their landlord wanted to double the restaurant's rent. But they had laid the groundwork to open

Interior of Bonne Soirée

their own French restaurant.

Upon leaving Kitty Hawk, they accepted an offer to open a restaurant in Raleigh. While there, they went to every part of the Triangle. At each stop, they played the what-if game. Finally, "we said Chapel Hill was it," recalls Chip.

They took the lessons they had learned from the three main chefs Chip had worked with and implemented them with loving care in Bonne Soirée. Add to that Chip's masterful cooking and Tina's palate in matching wines with food and her vision of a perfect French restaurant, and you get Chapel Hill's hidden gem.

Chip's cuisine has been described as "French with a Southern inflection." He grew up in Greenville and knows Southern food. But "I hate to pigeonhole it," Chip says of his cuisine. "It's French in theory, but not so much as, 'This is a French dish.' What we mean by *French* is that it's more European." It means, as Larry Forgione found out, buying fresh, local, seasonal ingredients, working with what is available, and keeping it simple.

On their trips to Europe, Chip and Tina noticed something else. The French cooks, whether at a truck stop or a three-star restaurant, did the best they could with what they had. "They do it because they love cooking," says Chef Chip. "They love life. Yes, there are hard times, but it's fun at the same time."

He adds, "Bonne Soirée is enough for us. We like our little restaurant. We come here, go home, make enough so we don't have to worry."

Chef Chip Smith's Recipes

Spot à la Basquaise

Serves 8

Spot

6 tablespoons peanut oil, divided
1 red pepper, diced small
1 yellow pepper, diced small
2 cups fresh field peas, blanched (pink-eyed, black-eyed, zipper, or crowder peas)
½ cup chicken stock
1 tablespoon butter
2 very ripe tomatoes, peeled, seeded, and diced small
2 green onions, thinly sliced
1 tablespoon mixed fresh herbs (thyme, rosemary, sage, parsley)
Salt and pepper to taste
Tabasco sauce to taste
8 spot fillets (or other small, delicate white pan fish with buttery flavor, such as croaker or butterfish)

Heat 2 tablespoons of the peanut oil in a medium sauté pan. Add red and yellow peppers and let sweat for 1 to 2 minutes. Add field peas and toss to coat in oil. Add chicken stock and butter and reduce until sauce forms a glaze on the vegetables. Add tomatoes, green onions, and fresh herbs. Season with salt and pepper and 1 or 2 drops of Tabasco. Toss to mix. Taste and adjust seasonings. Set aside and keep warm.

Heat a second sauté pan on high heat and add remaining 4 tablespoons of peanut oil. Season skin side of fillets with salt and pepper. When oil just begins to smoke, carefully place fillets in pan skin side down. Leave pan on high heat for a minute, then reduce heat to medium. Cook fillets for 3 to 4 minutes until they turn an opaque white. Turn fillets over and remove pan from heat. Let fillets gently finish cooking in pan off heat.

Sauce

½ cup white wine
6 tablespoons heavy cream
¼ cup piquillo peppers, chopped
¼ cup assorted peppers, chopped
Salt and pepper to taste
Juice of ½ lemon

Combine all ingredients in a saucepan, heat to medium, and reduce to a thin sauce.

To assemble, place field pea mixture on plates and place fish on top. Pour sauce on top or serve on the side.

POTS DE CRÈME AU CHOCOLAT
Serves 4

3 egg yolks
2½ tablespoons sugar
3 ounces Valhrona or other extra-bitter chocolate, finely
    chopped
1¾ cups heavy cream
6 tablespoons whole milk

Preheat oven to 300 degrees. In a bowl, whisk yolks and sugar. In a second bowl, add chocolate. In a medium pot, bring cream and milk just to a boil. Add half of the hot liquid to the chocolate. Pour remaining liquid in a very slow stream into yolk mixture, whisking constantly. Stir chocolate to blend completely with liquid. Gradually and slowly, add yolk mixture to chocolate, whisking to blend. Pour into four 8-ounce ramekins. Place in a baking pan with hot water halfway up sides of ramekins. Bake about 45 minutes until internal temperature is 170 to 175 degrees. Remove from oven and cool before serving.

Durham

Jim Anile

Jim Anile
at Revolution

Revolution
107 West Main St.
Durham, N.C. 27701
919-956-9999
info@revolutionrestaurant.com
www.revolutionrestaurant.com

Directions

From Raleigh, take I-40 West to Exit 279B. Go north on
Durham Freeway (N.C. 147) to Exit 14 (Swift Avenue/Duke
East Campus). At the end of the ramp, turn right at the light.
The next light is at Main Street. Turn right and continue for
about a mile to downtown Durham at Five Points. Stay on
Main Street. Revolution is on the right just past Corcoran
Street and SunTrust Bank. From Chapel Hill, take U.S. 15/501
Business (Durham–Chapel Hill Boulevard) to Exit 105A,
then follow U.S. 15/501 Bypass to Exit 108A. Take Durham
Freeway South to Exit 14 (Swift Avenue/Duke East Campus).
Turn left at the light and go to the second light, at Main Street.
Turn right and continue for about a mile to Five Points. Stay
on Main Street. Revolution is on the right just past Corcoran
Street and SunTrust Bank.

Cuisine

This chef-owned restaurant serves contemporary American
cuisine.

Executive Chef Jim Anile laid the groundwork for his new restaurant,
Revolution, in the late 1980s as a scruffy college student on a golf course,
when he met the men who changed his life. He showed up on the course
as a fill-in for a foursome, sporting his long hair, earrings, and combat
boots. When he was called to join a group, his new partners shuddered.
But "I ended up just killing them," Jim recalls. So, with new admiration,

Interior of Revolution

they asked him what he wanted to do with his life.

It turned out they worked at one of the Rosewood luxury boutique hotels in Dallas. As a student, Jim was undecided and open to possibilities. "I didn't know where my college studies were going," he says. He told the men that he had been cooking at his family's Italian restaurants and pizzerias and was at a pause in his pursuit of an international studies degree. One of the men said, "If you want a shot at cooking . . ."

Jim was offered a place in the employee dining room at one of the Rosewood Hotels. He remained at that level for two weeks. Within a year, he had his own dining room in the exclusive, members-only portion of the hotel. His career as a chef in boutique hotels had begun at the age of nineteen. And so he started his apprenticeship with European chefs and cooks.

Originally from Pennsylvania, Jim grew up in Texas, where his family had its businesses. He became enamored with food in his Italian family, which gathered as a large clan on Sundays. "Food was important in our family," he says. "Everyone worried about dinner first thing in the morning. 'What are you going to do about dinner?'"

Jim's family fostered his success in working with European chefs. "I grew up in a European family where everybody yelled, and it didn't intimidate me. The more they yelled, I put my head down and smiled and kept going. I knew it was nothing personal."

He continues, "That afforded me a lot of opportunities. There were all these Europeans, and nobody was used to their ways. But I was. I could let them scream at me three inches from my ear, and it didn't mean anything." He learned by apprenticing and staying at boutique hotels from the age of nineteen to thirty-five without actually looking for a job. "It's a very small network," he says.

Because of his connection with Rosewood Hotels early in his cooking career, he moved from one four- or five-star boutique hotel to another. He worked with chefs at the Melrose Hotel and the Crescent Club, both in Dallas. At age twenty-four, because of his connection to Chef Kevin Rathbun in Atlanta, he got the chance to work in Thailand, going back and forth between that nation and Dallas. His connection with Rosewood then led him to London's Lanesborough Hotel. He opened the Bacara Resort in Santa Barbara, California, and became executive chef at Yosemite National Park's Ahwahnee Hotel, built in the 1920s as luxury accommodations for national park donors. On all the moves, he took his wife and two children with him.

Jim's last boutique hotel was the Siena Hotel in Chapel Hill, where he was executive chef for six years at Il Palio. When the hotel management changed and his contract expired, he chose to stay in the area for two reasons. First, it was time to open his own restaurant. "I'd done it for everybody else, so I knew how to do it," he says. Second, his children were "starting to react to moving every four years."

Jim chose Durham as the site for his restaurant because he thought that "over the next ten years," the city would be "very different, especially downtown."

His plans for the restaurant started with the concept that it would be a revolution in the dining experience. He spent months developing a business plan and acquiring partners and the space, then further months working with contractors to develop the space in the Greenfire development's old Baldwin's department store on Main Street. Revolution is located near the base of the proposed luxury boutique hotel in the old CCB building, now owned by SunTrust. It is also near the Durham Performing Arts Center.

Jim created an environment conducive to both old-style fine dining and new-style relaxed dining. "We drew a line right down the middle of the restaurant. On one side, white tablecloths with four, five, six courses if you want; on the other, without the white tablecloths and three or four courses if you want. One side has really detailed service; the other is a more relaxed space, a place to stop by after work, have a couple of drinks, and go to the theater. That side is a little bit more comfortable, a little bit slick and modern. So the revolution is that you get to choose the environment that's comfortable to you," Jim says.

The basis of a great restaurant is smooth service and outstanding food. "Fundamentally, the food has to taste good," he says. His cuisine draws on his extensive experience in America, Asia, and Europe. He also brings in some techniques of molecular gastronomy—the application of scientific techniques and tools to cooking to create unusual and delicious versions of ordinary foods—but only when they make the cuisine taste better. Jim says, "I think that's one of the things that gets lost in the cool factor" associated with molecular gastronomy. "It has to work well."

His wine list is also part of the revolution. "The expensive wine list is gone. The focus in Revolution is on small producers with very interesting wine. It requires a lot of work on our part to teach the guests, to take the intimidation out. So we picked a number we can do—fifty," Jim says.

The menu changes constantly. "We want the best all the time," he says. "Instead of flying in a fish, since we have the ocean nearby, we'll fly in a tomato."

Jim says that "a chef is a boss of a team, and a great team lets you do the fun stuff—cooking. A great team makes a great restaurant."

His children are now in high school and elementary school. "We spent many a Christmas at a hotel. That's the only thing I really missed—the holidays," he says. Revolution is also changing Jim's own life. Thanks to the restaurant, he now knows when he has days off, Christmas being one.

Executive Chef Jim Anile's Recipes

SWEET PUMPKIN AND POPPY SEED CHUTNEY
Serves 10

½ tablespoon canola oil
1 whole shallot, chopped
1 jalapeño, seeded and chopped
1½ cups fresh pie pumpkin, diced small
1½ cups champagne vinegar

1 cup granulated sugar
1½ cinnamon sticks
2 whole star anise pods
½ tablespoon turmeric
1½ tablespoons plus 1 teaspoon poppy seeds
½ teaspoon salt, or to taste

Place a small saucepot over medium heat and add oil. Add shallot, jalapeño, and pumpkin. Lightly sauté for about 3 minutes. Deglaze pot with vinegar. Add sugar, cinnamon sticks, anise pods, turmeric, and poppy seeds and reduce liquid by ⅓. Season with salt.

Depending on acidity of champagne vinegar, you may need to add more salt. This will cut some of the harsh acid. You can also add more sugar if you like.

Serve chutney warm or at room temperature. Chutney can be made several days in advance. It is great with Thanksgiving turkey, ham, and leg of lamb.

ROASTED EGGPLANT AND WILD MUSHROOM SOUP

Serves 7 to 8

1 large eggplant
1½ teaspoons olive oil
3 cloves garlic, chopped
1 medium yellow onion, diced
1 stalk celery, chopped
1 medium potato, peeled and chopped
1 cup mushrooms, any kind
¼ cup Marsala
6 cups chicken broth or stock
⅓ cup heavy cream
1½ tablespoons balsamic vinegar
2 tablespoons grated Parmesan
Handful of fresh basil, tied in a bunch
Salt and pepper to taste

Preheat oven to 375 degrees. Rub eggplant with a little olive oil and place on a sheet pan in oven for 30 minutes. Cool, then peel and dice.

In a large soup pot, sauté garlic, onions, celery, potato,

and mushrooms in olive oil until onions are translucent and mushrooms have started to cook. Add eggplant and Marsala. When wine has cooked for 5 minutes, add chicken broth. Simmer covered for about 45 minutes until potatoes have cooked through. Turn heat to low, mix in cream and balsamic vinegar, and stir in Parmesan. Remove from heat and blend with an immersion blender until soup is smooth. Add basil and allow to steep for a few minutes before adding salt and pepper. (*Note:* The basil is essential.) Remove basil before serving. Top each soup bowl with croutons and grated cheese.

Drew Brown and Andy Magowan
at Piedmont

Piedmont
401 Foster St.
Durham, N.C. 27701
919-683-1213
info@piedmontrestaurant.com
www.piedmontrestaurant.com
Directions
> From Raleigh, take I-40 West to Exit 279B. Follow Durham
> Freeway North (N.C. 147) to the Swift Avenue/Duke East
> Campus exit. Turn right at the light and go to the second
> light, at Main Street. Turn right, follow Main Street to Five
> Points, and veer left onto West Chapel Hill Street. Go to the
> next stoplight and turn left onto Foster Street. Go past the
> next light to Piedmont, located on the left in a converted
> warehouse. From Chapel Hill, follow U.S. 15/501 Business
> (Durham–Chapel Hill Boulevard). Take Exit 105B onto
> U.S. 15/501 Bypass North. Go to Exit 108B and follow
> Durham Freeway South (N.C. 147) to Exit 14 (Swift Avenue/
> Duke East Campus). Turn left, go to the second stoplight, at
> Main Street, and follow the directions above.

Cuisine
> This chef-owned restaurant serves Italian cuisine featuring
> North Carolina produce. Everything is made in-house.

The Piedmont experience did not just happen. The two men who
created it out of their imaginations, Chef Drew Brown and Chef Andy
Magowan, wanted a restaurant that was different. Andy is particularly

Andy Magowan and Drew Brown

proud that "no other restaurant has all homemade foods," including those prepared through the craft of charcuterie. It is a practice he started at Federal in Durham. "Our food philosophy is to make comfort food from family experiences. Only we make the dishes better with high-quality ingredients," says Drew. "People should feel they're getting what they paid for. We assume a customer is not going to be wowed by that green drizzle on the plate."

He is too self-effacing. Piedmont's food is a complex, smooth blend of the finest, freshest ingredients, all prepared in a little kitchen. The restaurant Andy and Drew have created is greatly influenced by Michael Pollan's books, especially *The Omnivore's Dilemma*. "Our purveyors are local farmers. Being next to the Durham Farmers' Market is a big help," says Andy. At Piedmont, they offer meats, chicken, and eggs from local farmers, as well as fresh in-season produce. That's why the menu changes with the seasons.

The interior décor is "stylish, urban, simple. Not too much flair," says Drew. The striking outsized drawings on the walls are images made from Andy's collection of old botanical drawings. An artist friend projected the images on the walls and painted the line drawings in black on the beige and brick-red walls. The plants in the drawings, among them honeysuckle, are native to North Carolina.

Andy gives most of the credit for the success of Piedmont to Drew. In fact, it was Drew's meeting with Andy when he came back to Durham after a stint in Las Vegas at Thomas Keller's Bouchon that acted as a spark between the two. Andy was at that time the chef at Federal, where he made his reputation by turning the place into a pub that offered gourmet food. He prepared his own meat products through charcuterie, a skill that he has carried over to Piedmont. He also used fresh, locally grown ingredients. "The Federal was a bar with a kitchen in it. They brought me in and let me go. Let me do my thing," he says.

Andy had experience in a number of kitchens, including those at Magnolia Grill in Durham and La Résidence, Weaver Street Market, and Henry's Bistro in Chapel Hill. And he had spent a few months in London kitchens.

"I don't cut corners. I don't let anything go out that's subpar," Andy says. "I prefer classic French and Italian. I'm half Italian, and my mom is a really great cook."

Drew's experience in the food business began early. His obsession with food preparation was such that he got cookbooks instead of toys for Christmas and watched PBS cooking shows instead of cartoons. His parents owned a pizza parlor outside Columbus, Ohio.

His training as a cook came in some of Durham's better restaurants, where he worked under great chefs, picking up techniques from each of them. He worked at Pop's during the period when Chef Scott Howell of Nana's owned it. "It was staffed by all cooking-school students. Alton Brown worked there before he went on the Food Network. I got a sense of the fundamentals," says Drew. "It was at Pop's I got a sense that I really liked cooking."

Drew worked at Washington Duke Inn with then–executive chef Brian Ross, who had attended L'Academie de Cuisine in Washington, D.C. "He was an exceptional teacher. He turned me on to Escoffier and the French tradition. He taught me the fundamentals of pastry and baking. The bread at Piedmont is similar, made from a sour dough," he says.

He also worked for a time at Four Square with Chef Shane Ingram. "Good food," he recalls. Afterward, he occasionally went back to Four Square and asked the pastry chef how to make something.

A defining experience was his time working at Bouchon in Las Vegas under world-renowned chef Thomas Keller. Drew remembers seeing him just three or four times. But Chef Keller's staff had worked at the French Laundry and Bouchon in California's Napa Valley. "Keller was brilliant at building a staff and counting on them to do what he wanted them to do," says Drew.

Bouchon was the highlight of Drew's cooking career. "Up to that point, I wasn't that serious and never had a complete understanding of cooking. There, it all clicked." He arrived at the restaurant early and stayed late. Having no reason to do anything but work, he shared his passion for cooking with a fellow chef he eventually lured to Durham.

He never planned to return to Durham, but he wanted a place "a little less ridiculous than Las Vegas." And when he came back, he reconnected with an old acquaintance, Chef Andy Magowan, who was making his reputation as a great cook at Federal. And it was there that they imagined their restaurant.

Drew sums up his attitude, which is evident everywhere at Piedmont: "My nature is to want to craft an experience, a really positive one. Chef Andy and I both like to feed people. Like Andy's, my family is part Italian."

Dining area at Piedmont

Chef Drew's philosophy of cooking begins with "quality ingredients. Treat food with respect. Honor the craft. Take care of knives, tools. Keep the kitchen clean. Be aware of a cuisine's tradition. Know where the cuisine comes from and why we do things in a certain way. Have respect for the people who work for you. Customers are people coming into our home. Treat them with as much generosity as possible."

Chef Drew Brown and Chef Andy Magowan's Recipes

BRIOCHE BREAD PUDDING

Serves 10 to 12

1 dozen jumbo egg yolks
1 cup sugar
2 vanilla beans
1 quart heavy cream
1 loaf brioche

Preheat oven to 350 degrees. Whisk yolks and sugar to blend. Scrape seeds from vanilla bean pods and add to cream. (Pods may be reserved for future use.) Heat cream and vanilla to scalding. In a very slow stream, add cream to sugar and yolk mixture, whisking constantly. Strain.

Cut brioche into cubes and place in a 9-by-13-inch baking dish. Pour custard over brioche and cover with foil. Place baking dish in a roasting pan or other deep pan, add hot water halfway up baking dish, and bake for about 1 hour until pudding reaches 180 degrees.

"Serve as is for dessert with chocolate sauce and whipped cream, or allow to cool, then slice and fry for a very rich version of French toast—served with warm maple syrup, of course," Chefs Drew and Andy suggest.

SEARED SCALLOPS WITH BRAISED FENNEL, OLIVE OIL HOLLANDAISE, AND GRAPEFRUIT

Serves 4

Fennel

2 bulbs fennel
¼ cup extra-virgin olive oil
1 bottle white wine
1 lemon, sliced in half
2 bay leaves

Wash fennel bulbs and slice each into quarters. Leave roots intact. Roast in olive oil in a heavy saucepan until well caramelized. Add wine to just barely cover fennel. Add lemon and bay leaves and season to taste. Braise for 15 minutes or so. Fennel should be tender but not mushy. Set aside.

Hollandaise

1 cup extra-virgin olive oil
1 cup clarified butter
1 tablespoon Dijon mustard
2 tablespoons lemon juice
2 egg yolks
Salt and pepper

Warm olive oil and clarified butter. (To clarify butter, melt it in a saucepan. When melted, pour off clear butter fat, leaving behind milk solids and water.) In a bowl over a hot water bath, whisk Dijon, lemon juice, and yolks until thick and light. In a very slow stream, whisk in oil and butter to create an emulsion (a thick sauce). Season to taste.

This hollandaise may be refrigerated for 2 days.

Scallops

8 scallops
Salt and pepper to taste
1 tablespoon extra-virgin olive oil
1 grapefruit, segmented
Chives for garnish

Season scallops with salt and pepper, then sear them in olive oil. Cook to medium-rare, about 1 minute per side.

Place 2 quarters of fennel on each plate. Top with 2 scallops and drizzle on hollandaise. Place 2 grapefruit segments on top and garnish with a sprinkling of fresh chives.

Jason Cunningham
at Fairview
(Washington Duke Inn and Golf Club)

Fairview at Washington Duke Inn
and Golf Club
  3001 Cameron Blvd.
  Durham, N.C. 27705
  919-490-0999
www.washingtondukeinn.com
Directions
  From Raleigh, take I-40 East to Exit 270. Turn right
  and follow U.S. 15/501 Business (Durham–Chapel
  Hill Boulevard) toward Durham. Go to Exit 105B
  and follow U.S. 15/501 Bypass North. Go to Exit
  107, turn right, and follow Cameron Boulevard
  (N.C. 751) to the second light. Turn right into
  Washington Duke Inn and Golf Club, located
  opposite Science Drive. From Chapel Hill, take
  U.S. 15/501 Business toward Durham and follow the
  directions above.
Cuisine
  The restaurant at this AAA Four Star hotel serves
  Regional New American cuisine.

Executive Chef Jason Cunningham started out at Washington Duke
Inn as a line cook and, in a manner similar to his previous experiences,
took what he was given—an entry-level position—and rose to his current
role effortlessly. Now, he manages the entire food service at the inn, from

Jason Cunningham

the Fairview fine-dining restaurant to room service. On busy weekends such as Duke University's graduation and Mother's Day, he can be seen carrying around a clipboard with twenty sheets of paper outlining the coordination required.

He did not start out wanting to be executive chef of a luxury hotel. When he was thirteen in his hometown in Wisconsin, his parents encouraged him to get a job. The one he found was at a funeral home. He quickly left that and took a job washing dishes. One Thanksgiving, the chef-owner of the restaurant where he worked appeared in his white chef's coat and tall chef's hat carrying a huge roasted turkey on a platter. Chefs could be awe-inspiring, Jason realized.

By the time Jason went to Pennsylvania State University, his ambition was to be a doctor. Most likely, he would have accomplished that if he had not been responsible for rent, food, books, and tuition. To pay for those, he left school for a semester and took a job in a restaurant. Eventually, he decided to drop out of college and become a chef.

To pay for culinary school, he went to Raleigh, where his parents then lived, in order to save money. While there, he worked at Glenwood Grill, the same restaurant where Bret Jennings of Elaine's on Franklin had worked and Matthew Kelly of Vin Rouge would work. When the time came to choose a culinary school, he selected Johnson & Wales University in Charleston, South Carolina, because, for one thing, it was close to a beach. "I was in my twenties," Jason says. "I thought I knew everything."

The decision turned out to be an excellent one. For his externship, he worked at Charleston restaurants McCrady's and Restaurant Million, where he learned from Chef Jose de Anacleto.

"Culinary school was easy compared to working with the chef at Restaurant Million," Jason says. "I worked there for two years and learned about fine dining and classical French cuisine. This experience took everything to a whole different level."

After finishing at Johnson & Wales, he knew he needed to work with other great chefs to gain more experience, so he headed to Boston. Discovering that he could not work for ten dollars an hour and cover his debts from school, he took jobs with the small luxury inns Blantyre and Wheatleigh in western Massachusetts.

Luckily, the chef at Blantyre, Chef Michael Roller, had been *sous chef* at Restaurant Million, and most of the kitchen staff had come from Europe. "I was low man on the totem pole," says Jason, "but I learned so much from those guys. I was a sponge."

Then he worked at Wheatleigh with Chef Peter Platt. While there, "I got a call from a former student at Johnson & Wales," Jason says. "He asked me to be his *sous chef* at a hotel in Hawaii. It was a good time for me. It wasn't a career move, but it gave me time to set goals for myself." He spent eight or nine months there scuba-diving, spearfishing, catching rock lobsters, and camping.

He returned to North Carolina for two reasons: his father was sick, and he missed his dog. He stayed temporarily with his parents in Raleigh again. Coincidentally, his mother knew a woman who had a son-in-law who worked as banquet chef at Washington Duke Inn. That son-in-law told Jason there were openings. "So I applied," Jason says. Simple as that.

He began working at Washington Duke Inn in 2001 as a line chef. "In three weeks, I was promoted to *sous chef* and one year later to head chef at Fairview for breakfast, lunch, and dinner," he says. A year after that, the executive chef announced he was resigning and leaving for the West. "I threw my hat in the ring. I felt I could do the job," says Jason. "I knew I could do it. They gave me the job on a trial basis, and after six months the title." He is now responsible for the "whole food operation: banquets, Bull Durham Bar, Vista, Fairview, catering, and room service."

He describes his cuisine as "Regional New American." To Jason, this means that "we try to utilize indigenous ingredients such as collard greens, black-eyed peas, sweet potatoes. Yet we pull components from all regions of the country or the world. We're looking for different flavors. New American is the term used for drawing from all over the place and putting it together so it tastes good."

Jason describes himself as a perfectionist. "I make sure I communicate why a dish needs to be cooked a certain way. I'm demanding of myself because I want to make sure our guests get what they deserve, that we live up to our reputation." He adds, "It's all about the guests and what they take away."

Chef Jason is married, has two young children, and lives in West Raleigh. He is a featured chef in the 2008 cookbook *Great Chefs Cook Vegan*, by Linda Long.

Executive Chef Jason Cunningham's Recipes

RISOTTO OF WILD MUSHROOMS, ENGLISH PEAS, AND PARMESAN REGGIANO

Serves 3 to 4

2 to 3 quarts vegetable stock
½ cup unsalted butter
1 medium yellow onion, finely diced
1 tablespoon chopped fresh garlic
1½ cups Arborio rice
1½ cups fresh English peas, shelled (frozen peas may be substituted)
⅓ cup mixed wild mushrooms, minced
½ cup freshly grated Parmesan Reggiano
Salt and pepper to taste
Fresh parsley for garnish
Splash of truffle oil

Bring stock to a simmer in a saucepan, then turn off flame. Melt butter in a large saucepan over medium heat. Add onions and garlic and lightly sauté until tender. Add rice and stir to coat in butter. Allow rice to lightly toast over medium-low heat for about 5 minutes. Add 2 cups of the stock, return to a simmer, and stir rice thoroughly until most of the liquid is absorbed. Repeat this process, adding small amounts of stock and stirring constantly, until rice is nearly al dente. Blanch peas in salted boiling water for 3 minutes (1 minute for frozen peas), shock in ice water, drain, and reserve. Add mushrooms and more stock to risotto, stirring thoroughly. Rice should be tender but not soft. Add enough stock to give almost a soupy consistency. Add cheese and reserved peas and season with salt and pepper. Just before serving, finish risotto with parsley and garnish with more minced mushrooms and a splash of truffle oil.

Patio dining at Fairview

SAVORY BRINED AND GRILLED PORKCHOPS

Serves 2 to 4

2 cups water
½ cup kosher salt
½ cup brown sugar
1 bay leaf
2 juniper berries
½ teaspoon crushed red pepper
½ teaspoon dried thyme leaves
2 cups ice
2 to 4 double-cut pork loin chops, with or without bone
Salt and freshly ground pepper

Combine first 7 ingredients in a nonreactive pot and bring to a boil. Remove brine from heat and chill by adding ice. Makes 1 quart brine. Can be refrigerated up to 1 month.

Place porkchops in a bowl or baking dish. Pour enough cooled brine over chops to submerge them. Refrigerate for 4 hours, turning once. Remove chops from brine and discard liquid. Pat chops dry with a paper towel to remove excess brine. Season chops lightly with salt and pepper and grill over medium-high heat, turning every 3 to 5 minutes until an internal temperature of 150 degrees is reached.

Note: Brining helps to tenderize the meat and to impart or enhance flavor. Fairview brines its porkchops before lightly cold-smoking them. These chops are excellent served with grilled stone fruit (peaches or apricots).

Scott Howell

Scott Howell at Nana's

Nana's

2514 University Dr.
Durham, N.C. 27707
919-493-8469
info@nanasdurham.com
www.nanasdurham.com

Directions

From Raleigh, take I-40 West to Exit 270. Turn
right onto Chapel Hill Boulevard (U.S. 15/501
Business) and drive several miles to the stoplight at
James Street. Turn right, go one block to University
Drive, and turn right to Nana's.

Cuisine

This chef-owned restaurant serves French and
Italian cuisine with a Southern inflection.

Customers might see Scott Howell dressed in chef's whites, shorts,
and a baseball cap, delivering food to tables. Yet the executive chef and
owner of Nana's restaurant in Durham is one of the country's outstanding
chefs.

How did the Asheville native become a leading chef? His training,
the chefs he worked with, his increasingly sensitive palate, plus an early
home environment that usually included good food account for his
accomplishments.

Two Durham restaurants are the touchstones for all other restaurants in the area: Magnolia Grill and Nana's. Right after Nana's, named for Chef Scott's grandmother, opened in 1992, the feared and respected restaurant critic for *Esquire* magazine, John Mariani, named it one of the best new restaurants of 1993. The James Beard Foundation nominated Scott for Best Chef in the Southeast in 2008 and again in 2009. *Wine Spectator* has given Nana's its Award of Excellence. *Food & Wine* featured Scott and his recipes in 2001. These are just a few of Nana's recognitions.

His journey as a chef began in 1986 when Scott discovered he liked working in the kitchen. He was a line cook earning money for his education at Appalachian State University, from which he was about to graduate with a marketing degree. But he decided he liked cooking and set about finding the best cooking school. He was told it was the Culinary Institute of America in Hyde Park, New York. After finishing his last exam at Appalachian but before graduation ceremonies, he flew from Charlotte to New York and the Culinary Institute.

After his externships at the New York restaurants Jams and Arcadia, Scott went to Italy and worked for a year at San Domenico. But his most formative experience was his eighteen months with world-renowned chef David Bouley at his restaurant, Bouley. "Bouley was definitely the man, a brilliant guy and very challenging," says Scott. "Every day, I learned so much, though it was grueling. We would work from noon to 2 A.M."

Bouley had worked under Chef Joël Robuchon, "the best chef in the world," says Scott. "And Bouley was the first American to cook on line for Paul Bocuse. You don't often get the chance to work for people like that."

After working with Bouley, Scott went to California, where he worked for a year and a half with Chef Nancy Silverton, founder of La Brea Bakery.

Another important, high-ranking chef in Scott's training was Chef Ben Barker at Durham's Magnolia Grill, where Scott was *sous chef* for eighteen months.

"Bouley's cuisine is French and is most influential in developing my cuisine," says Scott, "but Ben Barker and I had a great relationship. From him, I learned about Southern food and Southern ingredients and how to work with wine." He adds, "It's a great friendship, though he's my competitor now."

Scott's approach to food is that it should be simple and use absolutely the best ingredients. "Fish should come out of the water yesterday." His

Interior of Nana's with Jane Filer's paintings

fresh meat is flown from New York or Atlanta. His produce is from local farmers, who deliver it daily.

Yet the central aspect of Scott's cuisine is technique. "It's a slower cooking process. Technique is what I'm striving for. The quality. Every time, I'm going to watch it being done," he says. "I've had to battle that aspect for more than seventeen years." He tells his staff, "This is how we do it here."

Scott is a perfectionist, like many great chefs. "I'm not accepting of something that's not right," he says. "I do have a streak like that. Mainly, I see things the way they should be. That's what I strive for."

Despite Scott's demand that things be right, or perhaps because of it, and despite the restaurant's reputation as one of the top two in Durham, if not the Triangle, Nana's is unpretentious. There are paintings on the walls by Carrboro's Jane Filer in an exuberant Latin or Caribbean style. Her paintings also hang at Pop's and the nearby Original Q Shack and Rockford Filling Station, courtesy of Scott.

Nana's space is divided into three small rooms, with the bar area separated by a low wall. The walls are painted wine red, clay, and mustard. The seating is upholstered benches and comfortable straight-backed chairs. In the bar, the tables are chest-high and big enough for either hors d'oeuvres or dinner.

"Some people wanted the restaurant to be pretentious. I'm not going to let that happen," says Scott.

Though he has no plans for a cookbook, he does have a new eatery. Rockwood Filling Station, named for the former occupant of the building, is a few doors down from Nana's and next door to the Original Q Shack. "It's designed to accommodate wood-burning pizza, which is what I wanted Pop's to be in the first place." (Scott owned Pop's in downtown Durham before John Vandergrift and Chris Stinnett, former workers at Nana's, bought it.) Scott's longtime barkeeper, John Riggs, runs Rockwood Filling Station. Occasionally, Scott can be seen serving the customers. "It'll be the last restaurant I'll do for a while," he says.

Several notable chefs have come from Chef Scott's kitchen, including Sarig Agasi, Dan Ferguson, Ashley Christensen, Seth Kingsbury, and Tom Ferguson, among others.

Since 1992, Scott Howell has maintained the high quality and rigorous standards that continue to make Nana's an exceptionally fine and welcoming restaurant.

Executive Chef Scott Howell's Recipes

SWEET POTATO GRATIN WITH PRUNES
Serves 12

2 tablespoons unsalted butter
1½ pounds Vidalia onions, finely chopped
2 tablespoons chopped thyme
Salt and freshly ground pepper to taste
2 cups heavy cream
½ pound plump prunes, pitted
6 pounds sweet potatoes

Preheat oven to 350 degrees. Butter a 4-quart glass or ceramic baking dish.

Melt butter in a large saucepan and add onions and thyme. Season with salt and pepper. Cover and cook over medium heat about 5 minutes until onions soften. Uncover and cook until liquid has evaporated. Add cream and bring to a boil, then remove from heat. When cooled, strain onions, reserving onions and cream separately. Spread prunes between sheets of plastic wrap and flatten them to ¼-inch thickness with a meat pounder or rolling pin. Peel sweet potatoes and slice to ⅛-inch thickness. In a large bowl, toss ¾ of the sliced sweet potatoes with prunes and onions. Season with salt and pepper. Place sweet potatoes, prunes, and onions in buttered baking dish. Arrange remaining sweet potato slices on top in a decorative pattern. Pour reserved cream evenly over sweet potatoes. Cover baking dish with buttered parchment paper and then foil. Bake for 45 minutes or longer until sweet potatoes are tender, bubbling, and golden brown.

SWEET AND SOUR VIDALIA ONION RELISH
Makes about 1½ cups

2 tablespoons unsalted butter
2 large Vidalia onions, halved lengthwise and thinly sliced

2 tablespoons sugar
½ cup golden raisins
½ cup red wine vinegar
1 tablespoon Campari
Salt and freshly ground pepper to taste

Melt butter in a large saucepan. Add onions, cover, and cook about 15 minutes over medium-low heat, stirring occasionally until softened. Uncover, add sugar, and cook for 10 to 15 minutes, stirring frequently, until onions are very tender and lightly browned. Stir in raisins, vinegar, and Campari and season with salt and pepper. Cook uncovered over medium-low heat for about 10 minutes until most of the liquid evaporates. Transfer to a bowl and allow to cool. Serve at room temperature.

This relish can be refrigerated for up to 5 days.

Shane Ingram
at Four Square

Four Square
2701 Chapel Hill Rd.
Durham, N.C. 27707
919-401-9877
info@foursquarerestaurant.com
www.foursquarerestaurant.com

Directions

From Raleigh, take I-40 West to Exit 270 toward Durham and turn right to follow U.S. 15/501 Business (Durham–Chapel Hill Boulevard). Stay on U.S. 15/501 Business to the exit for N.C. 751/Duke University. Turn left at the exit stoplight, go one block to Pickett Road, turn right, and stay on Pickett Road until it dead-ends at Chapel Hill Road. Four Square is directly ahead. From Chapel Hill, take U.S. 15/501 Business toward Durham and follow the directions above.

Cuisine

This AAA Four Diamond restaurant serves globally influenced Contemporary American cuisine using local seasonal produce. The chef and his wife own and operate Four Square.

Chef Shane Ingram and his wife and partner, Elizabeth Woodhouse, now have the restaurant of their dreams. Named the area's most romantic restaurant by Citysearch, Four Square came to fruition only through years of training and honing of skills.

Shane, after a brief stint in casino hotels, knew he wanted to work

Shane Ingram

with the best chefs around. So he set out to find them. Without a job, he drove from New Jersey to New Orleans—"one of the great culinary cities," he says. There, after five interviews, he ended up working side by side with Emeril. "All experience is good," Shane says. "When I was with Emeril, he had only one restaurant, and he was in it every day. Great experience. He's quite a guy. Not what you see on TV now."

But living in New Orleans was not great. Shane then went to Seattle, where he worked at Le Tastevin, an old French restaurant past its prime and "no longer great," he says. Even though he loved the city, he stayed with his goal—to work with the best. He called Emeril and asked for a letter recommending him to Chicago's Charlie Trotter.

He worked in Chicago for a little over two years. "At Trotter's, I worked every station. There was no talking in the kitchen. No stopping. We ate on the go. Fourteen-, sixteen-hour days. Just powered through it. Hard. Really hard," Shane says. "But the great part of working for Charlie was that every day I learned something."

For Shane, Emeril and Charlie Trotter were equally influential. "They were teachers of life," he says. "Charlie would say, 'Hope you're not going out tonight. Hope you're going home to read.' He gave us copies of Ayn Rand or *Moby Dick*. He wanted us to read about food, to be happy, to be good people. I wish I could still talk with those guys, but their time is so chopped up now."

After his time at Charlie Trotter's, he went to what he calls "the most famous restaurant in America," The Inn at Little Washington in Washington, Virginia, to work with Chef Patrick O'Connell. "It's famous because of how they treat their customers, how they treat the town." He was there for a year. It was at The Inn at Little Washington that he met Elizabeth, a pastry chef. They married and took off on a food and wine tour of Europe.

"I would not have been able to do what I've done without Elizabeth," says Shane. She is the general manager at Four Square and holds an MBA from the University of Texas and a degree from the Culinary Institute of America.

The two of them researched areas where they could pursue their dream of owning a restaurant. They found that the Triangle was expected to "blow up" and chose Durham as their site. Once there, Shane worked at Fearrington House and Elizabeth worked as general manager for two other restaurants, preparing for the day they would own their own restaurant.

Interior of Four Square

After two years of searching, they found the 1908 Bartlett Mangum House and its massive Doric columns. The fact that the house had been used as a restaurant in the 1970s and 1980s made it ideal for their plans. Because the kitchen was equipped and the house already had tables and chairs, Shane and Elizabeth managed to open their restaurant after only two months of intensive labor.

They named it Four Square to reflect the classic balance and the lack of pretense of the house and their restaurant. Their opening date in October 1999 is important to Shane because one of his goals was to have an operating restaurant for ten years. They celebrate their ten-year anniversary on October 5, 2009.

"Every day, I come out to the dining room and I meet new people. So our business is expanding, but our base is the customer who has been with us all these years. We're close to them," says Shane. "Our customers are happy people. They're on a night out. They drink a little wine. A happy time. What could be better than that? Being with your friends, working, cooking. That makes us happy."

The third member of their team is Brandon Carr, the maître d'hôtel and sommelier, who has been with Shane and Elizabeth since the opening of Four Square. "What impresses me the most about Brandon," says Shane, "is his palate, his ability to match our food with the right wine."

Four Square's cuisine reflects Shane's philosophy of food. "We need to purchase from the people around us, to use local farmers and purveyors. Our job is to buy locally, to get the freshest products, to work with these guys," he says. "I hope it'll always be this way in this restaurant, in all restaurants."

To reflect the changing seasons and changing produce and other local products, Shane changes the menu monthly. "Customers come in expecting the unexpected," he says. The wait staff has a monthly tasting of every item on the menu so they can be most helpful to customers.

The Durham Farmers' Market plays a key role in Four Square's cuisine. "It makes me happy to be at the farmers' market. It's like my third home, after my real home and the restaurant," he says.

"There's something about being a cook. You work till midnight. You get up and do it the next day. Cooks are close-knit. We feed off that pressure. That stress. That adrenaline. That's what we like about it," says Shane.

And that leads to the ability to be creative. "Food is art," he says. "An expression of yourself. That's one of the true joys of my life. Expressing yourself in your food. If you're mad or happy or sad, it should show itself in your food. A beautiful day. Everything. That's the way to present in the dining room."

Creativity is one of the things he demands from his cooks. "Cooks like to be led, to be told what to do. I tell them, 'I have you here to be creative.' "

Several cooks have gone on from the Four Square kitchen to open their own restaurants. Drew Brown opened Piedmont. Matthew Kelly is at Vin Rouge. Andres Macias is at Tonali. Others have made names for themselves as well. "When people in the kitchen go off and do their own thing, it's a sign of a healthy restaurant," says Chef Shane.

Executive Chef Shane Ingram's Recipes

SOUTHERN FIELD PEA SALAD
Serves 6 to 8

Vinaigrette
½ cup blended olive oil
6 tablespoons apple cider vinegar
1 teaspoon whole-grain mustard
1½ teaspoons honey

In a small bowl, slowly whisk olive oil into vinegar until mixture thickens and is blended. Whisk in mustard. Whisk in honey.

Salad
1 cup fresh field peas, blanched
2 apples, peeled, cored, and diced small
1 onion, grilled and diced small
1 teaspoon minced garlic
1 teaspoon minced shallot
2 ribs celery, diced small
1 teaspoon finely chopped chives

1 teaspoon finely chopped parsley
Salt and pepper to taste

In a large bowl, combine field peas, apples, onions, garlic, shallots, and celery. Mix in vinaigrette. Add chives and parsley and season with salt and pepper.

Fig Gazpacho

Serves 8

3 red tomatoes, peeled, seeded, and diced small
3 yellow tomatoes, peeled, seeded, and diced small
2 green zebra tomatoes, peeled, seeded, and diced small
Salt to taste
2 baby leeks, white parts only, minced
3 cloves garlic, peeled and minced
1 green bell pepper, seeded and finely chopped
1 yellow bell pepper, seeded and finely chopped
2 hot chili peppers, seeded and minced
Juice of 2 limes
2 to 4 tablespoons habanero sauce
3 tablespoons *ponzu* (Japanese citrus) juice or lemon or grapefruit juice
¼ cup extra-virgin olive oil
1 pint brown turkey figs, quartered
Chopped cilantro to taste
Chopped basil to taste
Chopped chives to taste

Place tomatoes in a bowl and add salt. Combine leeks, garlic, bell peppers, and chilies in a large mixing bowl. Add lime juice, hot sauce, and *ponzu* and let sit for 5 minutes. Add tomatoes and olive oil. Just before serving, so they will not break down too quickly, add figs and herbs. Season with salt. Taste and adjust seasonings.

Matthew Kelly

Matthew Kelly
at Vin Rouge

Vin Rouge
2010 Hillsborough Rd.
Durham, N.C. 27705
919-416-0466
www.ghgrestaurants.com

Directions

Vin Rouge is at the corner of Ninth Street and
Hillsborough Road in Durham, next to Blu Seafood
and Bar. From Raleigh, take I-40 West to Exit 279B and
follow N.C. 147 North (Durham Freeway) to Exit 14
(Swift Avenue/Duke East Campus). Turn right at the
light and go to the second light, at Main Street. Continue
across Main Street onto Broad Street and go to the third
stoplight, at Markham Avenue. Turn left onto Markham
and go to the next light, at Ninth Street. Vin Rouge is
across the street to the right. From Chapel Hill, take U.S.
15/501 Business (Durham–Chapel Hill Boulevard) to
Exit 105B, then follow U.S. 15/501 Bypass North to Exit
108B (Durham Freeway South/N.C. 147). Go to Exit
14 (Swift Avenue/Duke East Campus). Turn left at the
light. Continue past Main Street onto Broad Street and
go to the third stoplight, at Markham Avenue. Turn left
onto Markham and go to the next light, at Ninth Street.
Vin Rouge is across the street to the right.

Cuisine

This chef-owned restaurant operating in partnership with
Giorgios Bakatsias serves French Bistro cuisine.

"It's a celebration," says Chef Matthew Kelly. His restaurant, Vin Rouge, the French bistro at the intersection of Hillsborough and Ninth streets in Durham, reflects his exuberant personality. The restaurant's Red Room is a small room with lace over the lighting fixtures, pristine white tablecloths, and, of course, red walls. It is noisy when filled with diners. Matt says, "Noisy is the nature of a French bistro. So many different types of people are there. They all get along and have a good time. It's about celebration. It's about quick food."

The bistro dates from the early nineteenth century. Though the origin of the word is in question, Matt says it is from the Russian *bystro,* meaning quick. "We're a neighborhood bistro, and that has been around for a long time. We have to pay homage to that tradition."

He pays homage through careful monitoring of details, like having the right serving dishes for the food, carefully replicating traditional foods like *steak frites,* and purchasing the best products he can find.

"Our food is served on special plates—cast iron, mussel bowls. By doing that, we're paying homage to a tradition," he says. "And I cook the traditional recipes in the best, most consistent way I can."

In a bistro, food and wine are not considered separately. Matt's manager, Michael Maller, is his *sommelier,* or wine steward. "He's open to new flavors of wine and has a great palate. Maller listens to the guests, saying, 'Tell me what you want, and I'll give it to you.'"

Matt graduated from the Culinary Institute of America and trained with some of the most revered chefs on the East Coast. He worked with Patrick O'Connell at The Inn at Little Washington, a five-star restaurant in Washington, Virginia; at Fearrington House Restaurant, a AAA Five Diamond restaurant in Pittsboro; at Fins in Raleigh; and at other high-quality restaurants. "You don't just learn from the chef. You learn from the entire experience," he says.

One of the most important things he learned was that he "didn't want to live it." Five-star restaurants aim at perfection with each dish, so there is a high focus on that dish. "I wanted more balance in my life."

Giorgios Bakatsias, owner of eight restaurants in the Triangle, contacted Chef William D'Auvray at Fins in Raleigh and indicated he was looking for a chef for his bistro, Vin Rouge. At the time, Matt was working at Fins and thinking about opening a French bistro. He and Giorgios got together. The match has had outstanding consequences.

The first four or five days at Vin Rouge were hard. But after that, with a

Interior of Vin Rouge

staff he hired and trained and with fine food equal to the name *bistro*, Matt turned the flailing restaurant around.

Since that time more than six years ago, "the menu has grown and expanded, as has the staff. There are fifty-two seats in the restaurant, and on a Friday night there can be one hundred eighty-seven people served."

Though Matt spent a great deal of his childhood in Raleigh and New Jersey, he always went back to the place he calls home—Upstate New York. "It's a really small town. The food was delicious, plentiful bounty," he says. "My family is Irish, and I like to do family dinners where things are passed on. My grandfather made a stuffing that we try to replicate. I can't wait till I finally get it down."

He loves to eat. He loves food. He's committed to being the best chef he can be.

"What's a chef's job?" he asks, then answers the question himself. "The really important job of a chef is to provide healthy, safe, nutritious food. We have to pay homage to the food that comes in here," he says. "I tell my cooks, 'This plant was pulled out of the ground. Let's be good to it. This animal was slaughtered. Let's do something good with it so people can enjoy it.'"

He adds, "Chefs always want to make everyone happy. If one person out of two thousand said the portions are too small, I make them larger."

Vin Rouge has become a successful French bistro under Matt's management. It reflects his joy at being there. "I really enjoy what I do. I love cooking. I'm very thankful I get to do something I love and I get paid for it. I don't even call it a job," he says.

He's proud of the restaurant's categorization. "We're not a North Carolina regional restaurant. We're not a French restaurant with little portions. We're a French bistro." His enthusiasm carries over to the whole experience that guests have at Vin Rouge. They thrive, and the staff thrives on their enjoyment.

"I appreciate that people like to come to this restaurant. I'm thrilled," Chef Matt says. "As long as people enjoy themselves and like to come back, that's a huge compliment for my entire staff. We're really happy to be part of a community that has good restaurants. It's awesome that people like to come here."

Chef Matthew Kelly's Recipes

CREAMED SPINACH

Serves 6

1 quart half-and-half
1 clove garlic, chopped
½ teaspoon freshly grated nutmeg
Salt and pepper to taste
2½ pounds baby flat-leaf spinach
2 sticks unsalted butter
¾ cup flour
1 to 2 ounces Gruyère cheese, grated
Heavy cream to drizzle

Preheat oven to 400 degrees. In a large pot, bring half-and-half just to a boil. Add garlic, nutmeg, salt, and pepper. Working in batches, stir in spinach just until wilted. Continue stirring in more spinach until all 2½ pounds have been incorporated into cream mixture. Remove from heat. Make a roux by melting butter in a sauté pan over medium heat and stirring in flour. Continue stirring until mixture thickens and forms gravy. Remove from heat. Add roux to spinach, return to heat, and bring to a boil. Stir until roux thickens the cream and spinach mixture. Using an immersion blender, lightly pulse until ingredients are just mixed but not puréed. Adjust seasonings. Place spinach in an ovenproof serving container. Sprinkle with Gruyère and drizzle heavy cream on top. Bake for 6 to 8 minutes until cheese is golden brown.

OYSTERS GRATIN

Serves 6

24 oysters packed in liquid
2 sticks butter
1 onion, diced
2 leeks, diced
2 cups sliced mushrooms
½ cup flour

1 quart milk
1 tablespoon dried tarragon
Tabasco sauce to taste
Lemon juice to taste
Salt and pepper to taste
2 slices bacon, cooked and chopped
2 ounces Gruyère cheese, shredded
3 tablespoons heavy cream

Place oysters in a pan and poach in their own liquid for about 2½ minutes until lips start to curl. Reserve. Melt butter in a large saucepan. Sweat onions in butter. Add leeks and mushrooms. Stir in flour and then milk. Bring to a boil. Add tarragon, Tabasco, lemon juice, salt, and pepper. Add mixture to a warm serving pan. Add oysters and liquid from oysters and bring mixture to desired consistency. Finish with bacon, then cheese on top. Drizzle cream on top. For color, place under broiler for 30 to 45 seconds until brown and bubbly.

Tim Lyons
at Blu Seafood and Bar

Blu Seafood and Bar
2002 Hillsborough Rd.
Durham, N.C. 27705
919-286-9777
info@bluseafoodandbar.com
www.bluseafoodandbar.com

Directions

Blu Seafood and Bar is at the corner of Ninth Street
and Hillsborough Road in Durham, next to Vin Rouge.
From Raleigh, take I-40 West to Exit 279B and follow
N.C. 147 North (Durham Freeway) to Exit 14 (Swift
Avenue/Duke East Campus). Turn right and go to
the fourth stoplight, at Markham Avenue. Turn left
and go to the next light, at the corner of Ninth Street.
The restaurant is across the street on the right. From
Chapel Hill, take U.S. 15/501 Business (Durham–
Chapel Hill Boulevard) to Exit 105B, then take U.S.
15/501 Bypass North to Exit 108B (Durham Freeway
South/N.C. 147) and follow the directions above.

Cuisine

This chef-owned restaurant serves fresh seafood,
meats, and salads.

Luckily for diners in the Triangle, Chef Tim Lyons and his family
escaped Key West after the intense storm surge of Hurricane Wilma in
2005 just about devastated the town. After looking around for a place
to resettle, he chose Durham as the site where he would open a seafood

Tim Lyons

restaurant like no other that Triangle residents had seen before—unless they were visitors to Key West. And so his coast-to-coast journey from childhood in Huntington Beach, California, to his seven years at Louie's Backyard in Key West brought him to Durham.

Tim was ten years old when Chef Roland Gaujac married his sister and introduced him to the world of fine cuisine. The couple's first child was born in Paris, and the Lyons family traveled through Europe for the baptism, eating along the way. Then, when Tim graduated from high school, he went to Chef Gaujac's place in Vermont—Roland's Place 1796 House—to help get the guesthouse ready to open.

Gaujac taught him about fresh sauces and the authentic French style of cooking, techniques Tim uses today. After a while, Tim realized he wanted to have his own place but lacked the experience to open one. He set about acquiring that experience by working with some of the best chefs in the country, such as Swedish chef Gustaf Anders, whose namesake restaurant is ranked as one of the nation's top fifty. Tim was *sous chef* for Chef Anders, from whom he learned the art of refinement.

His most telling experience came when he worked with Chef Doug Shook at Louie's Backyard in Key West. Fresh ingredients and a simple style were the mainstays at the restaurant and a lasting part of Tim's training. At Louie's Backyard, where he was *sous chef* under Chef Shook, he implemented all his previous training and experience.

But the hurricane prompted him to leave a city he loved and find a site conducive to the seafood restaurant he had in mind. "Chefs were saying that the Triangle was starting to blow up," he says. "I looked at six or seven places, and I liked this area. There are a lot of foodies here who like to try new things."

He opened Blu Seafood and Bar—named after the blue sea he so loves—two years after the hurricane. His seafood is excellent, fresh, and even exotic. Tim has his seafood sent via Fed Ex from far away in his effort to find the best fish and oysters. He brings in fish from Hawaii via the Honolulu Fish Company ("Their fish is immaculate, the freshest," he says); from Miami and Atlanta via Inland Seafood; and from Southport Seafood and small, independent sources along the North Carolina coast. He serves fish from Hawaii, Greece, Europe, the Gulf Coast, and the Eastern Seaboard.

"Oysters are a big thing for Blu," Tim says. "There are Gulf Coast oysters, from Florida and Louisiana. And there are cold-water oysters

Bar at Blu Seafood and Bar

from Canada—the Beausoleil—and Massachusetts blue points. Cold-water oysters are brinier, saltier." Blu specializes in cold-water oysters, which Tim serves on the half shell, fried, or baked.

He will special-order any kind of oyster or fish. "If someone says, 'I like this kind of oyster or seafood,' I'll try to bring it in. Need a day's notice, but I'll try my hardest." He prepares his seafood simply, bringing out its fresh taste.

The fresh seafood is a large part of Blu's attraction. But two other characteristics of the restaurant have attracted a growing number of guests. The entire staff contributes, first, to the Key West atmosphere and, second, to the principle that guests will be known and welcomed into Blu.

"Guests are the big thing with us. We do our best to know their names. The manager, Eryk Pruitt, does a really good job of keeping in contact with them. We don't like front-of-the-house pretentiousness, where the restaurant expects guests to thank them," says Chef Tim. "We should be thanking them." He wants to make Blu feel like an upscale neighborhood place with outstanding food.

Blu Seafood and Bar regularly has special oyster nights, wine nights, a happy hour, and other special events and celebrations.

Chef Tim Lyons's Recipes

SALSA VERDE

"At Blu, we use salsa verde to brush on our whole fish as it roasts in the oven. However, it can be used on steaks, chicken, and vegetables, even pasta," Chef Tim says.

Yields 1½ cups

½ bunch parsley
½ bunch cilantro
½ bunch basil
4 cloves garlic
1 shallot
2 tablespoons capers
4 anchovy fillets
½ cup blended oil
½ cup extra-virgin olive oil

Place first 7 ingredients and half the oil in a blender or food processor. Purée until smooth. Slowly add remaining oil.

Mango-Pecan Brown Butter

"At Blu, we serve it with North Carolina rainbow trout," Chef Tim says.

Yields ½ cup

1½ tablespoons unsalted butter
2 tablespoons diced mango
1 tablespoon chopped pecans
Juice from ½ lemon
1 tablespoon chopped parsley
Salt and pepper to taste

In small saucepan, melt butter until brown. Add mangoes and pecans. Remove from heat. Add lemon juice, parsley, salt, and pepper. Immediately pour over fish of your choice.

Stone-Ground Grits with Sharp Cheddar

Serves 6 to 8

1 cup white stone-ground grits
2 cups water
2 cups whole milk
2 cups shredded Vermont cheddar cheese
½ teaspoon cayenne pepper
1 tablespoon unsalted butter
Salt and pepper to taste

Add grits, water, and milk to a large saucepan. Turn heat on medium. As mixture warms, stir frequently so grits do not stick to bottom of pan. Once grits are warm, turn heat to low. Never let mixture come to a rapid boil. Cook grits 40 to 60 minutes until desired thickness is reached. Once grits are creamy and not crunchy, turn heat off and add cheese, cayenne, and butter. Taste and season with salt and pepper.

Andres Macias
at Tonali

Tonali

3642 Shannon Rd.
Durham, N.C. 27707
919-489-8000

Directions

From Raleigh, take I-40 West to Exit 270. Turn right
toward Durham on U.S. 15/501 Business (Durham–
Chapel Hill Boulevard) and continue past Target to
Shannon Road. Turn right and go past three stoplights
to Tonali, located just before the post office. From
Chapel Hill, take U.S. 15/501 Business to Durham. Go
past Target to Shannon Road. Turn right and go past
three stoplights to Tonali, just before the post office.

Cuisine

This chef-owned restaurant serves classic Mexican
cuisine made with local produce and cheeses.

Chef Andres Macias had no intention of opening another Tex-Mex
restaurant where rice and beans were the main ingredients. "I believe
Mexican cuisine is about freshness, using good-quality meat and chicken.
Others have presented us with a very different kind of Mexican cuisine,"
he says.

His dream was to open a restaurant that featured true, traditional

Andres Macias

Mexican cuisine. He made that passion come true, presenting to the public authentic Mexican food, the kind mothers and grandmothers make, the kind found in the better restaurants in Mexico.

He named his restaurant Tonali, an Aztec word that means "awakening of the soul." It's the symbol of the sun in Aztec writing. "I decided to do a tribute to what I believe is part of my culture," Andres says.

In pursuing traditional Mexican cuisine, he uses "what is local here. I make some visits to farms to be sure there are no chemicals, no pesticides being used," he says. "I go to the Durham Farmers' Market and also to the ones in Carrboro and Raleigh."

The specialty Mexican items "must follow my expectations—be as much natural as possible. I get *moles* [complex sauces] from Chihuahua, chilies from Jalisco, traditional herbs such as *hoja santa*, or holy leaf, and *epozate* from purveyors in Atlanta and San Diego," he says.

"Elodie Farms does our cheeses. He's an amazing friend. He produces for us *queso fresco* and *queso blanco*. We now have goat cheese introduced in the menu," Andres says. "Whatever he's got ready."

In being true to classic Mexican cuisine, he uses "fresh, light, local produce in season." And to ensure he gets what he requires, he is "developing our own garden in back of the restaurant."

Before Andres began to pursue his dream of recovering authentic Mexican cuisine, he had a passion for French and Japanese food. Though he worked with several chefs, the two most influential in his career and whose lessons have been implemented at Tonali are Chef Shane Ingram at Four Square in Durham and Chef Masa at Waraji restaurant in Raleigh.

Andres was *sous chef* at Four Square for five years. "Shane is a mentor. He changed my life. He was always someone I admired and trusted," Andres says. He learned many lessons from Shane Ingram: "Never cut corners. Visit farmers. Talk to purveyors. Support nature."

Masa is the chef-owner of Waraji, "one of the best Japanese restaurants in the Triangle," says Andres. "I did a *stage* every Monday, my day off. It was a great honor to be a part of that culture." From Masa, he learned not to have large plates and to create balance. "Whatever you have learned comes into your cooking," he says.

Andres was a painter as a youth, and some of his works hang in the restaurant. But "when you grow older, you have different commitments. And my commitment was to my children," he says. He has three girls.

When he came to the United States from Mexico more than twenty-one years ago, he expected to be an engineer, "but cooking won my heart. I dream about cooking," Andres says. He keeps numerous reference books beside his bed—books by Patricia Quintana, Martha Ortiz Chapa, Diana Kennedy (with whom he worked), Thomas Keller, and Charlie Trotter, among others.

Tonali has become a canvas where Chef Andres "can work with traditional ingredients to create traditional dishes," he says. "The texture, the colors of Mexico."

Interior of Tonali

Chef Andres Macias's Recipes

TONALI SALSA CHINTEXTLE
Yields 2 cups

5 dried pasilla peppers,* rinsed
1 ounce dried shrimp,* rinsed
4 avocado leaves*
4 xoconoxtles* (a type of sour prickly pear)
1 small clove garlic, peeled
¼ cup pumpkin seeds
¾ cup or more pineapple juice, cider vinegar, or water
Salt and freshly ground pepper to taste

*These ingredients can be found in Mexican grocery stores.

Cut tops off peppers and halve lengthwise. Remove seeds.
Place peppers in a skillet and roast until soft and browned. Set
aside. Repeat separately with dried shrimp, avocado leaves,
xoconoxtles, garlic, and pumpkin seeds. Roast each to a nice
color, making sure not to burn. When xoconoxtles are done,
cut in half and remove seeds, leaving just flesh. Place above
ingredients in a food processor or blender and mix until a
smooth, thick paste forms. Add pineapple juice, cider vinegar,
or water to bring to desired consistency. Add salt and pepper.
This sauce can be used on many foods, including the tamale
cakes below.

MEXICAN CORN TAMALE CAKES
Yields 8 to 10 cakes

¾ stick butter
1 tablespoon white onion, finely diced
1 clove garlic, finely chopped
½ poblano pepper, roasted, cleaned, seeded, and finely
    chopped
1½ cups milk

½ cup chicken stock or water
¾ cup stone-ground hominy or stone-ground grits
¼ cup tamale masa harina or white cornmeal (can be found in
    Mexican grocery stores)
Small bunch fresh cilantro, chopped
½ cup fresh goat cheese (optional)
Juice of 1 lime
Salt and freshly ground pepper to taste

Place butter in a pot. Incorporate onions, garlic, and poblano. Sauté over low heat about 2 minutes until caramelized. Add milk and stock. Increase heat for about 5 minutes until a slow boil is reached. Slowly add hominy or grits and masa harina or cornmeal. Using a wooden spoon to incorporate dry ingredients, stir constantly to avoid lumps. Reduce heat to a simmer and cook for about 15 minutes. Continue mixing from time to time in 1 direction until mixture reaches a smooth consistency. Add liquid if needed to bring to desired thickness. Add cilantro, goat cheese if desired, lime juice, and salt and pepper. Pour mixture over a lightly greased half sheet tray or casserole pan and let cool. Cut into 8 or 10 cakes. Remove cakes from pan and place in a skillet over low heat, adding oil as necessary. Caramelize both sides. Place in a 325-degree oven for about 5 minutes to finish.

Chris Stinnett and John Vandergrift at Pop's: A Durham Trattoria

Pop's: A Durham Trattoria

810 West Peabody St.
Durham, N.C. 27701
919-682-8844
john@pops-durham.com or chris@pops-durham.com
www.pops-durham.com

Directions

From Raleigh, take I-40 West to Exit 279B. Follow Durham Freeway North (N.C. 147) to Exit 14 (Swift Avenue/ Duke East Campus). Turn right at the stoplight and go to the next light, at Main Street. Turn right and continue to Gregson Street at the corner of Brightleaf Square. Turn right, go one block to Peabody Street, and turn left. Go half a block to Pop's, on the left. From Chapel Hill, take U.S. 15/501 Business (Durham–Chapel Hill Boulevard) to Exit 105A, then follow U.S. 15/501 Bypass to Exit 108A, then take Durham Freeway South (N.C. 147) to Exit 14 (Swift Avenue/Duke East Campus). Turn left at the light and go to the second light, at Main Street. Turn right and continue to Gregson Street at the corner of Brightleaf Square. Turn right, go one block to Peabody Street, and turn left. Go half a block to Pop's, on the left.

Cuisine

Pop's two chefs own this restaurant, which serves Italian trattoria-style food.

Chris Stinnett and John Vandergrift

Chef Chris Stinnett thrives on Durham, which in turn helps make his and Chef John Vandergrift's restaurants—Pop's: A Durham Trattoria and Rue Cler—thrive. Chris became fascinated with food when he watched his grandfather, a butcher, stand at the kitchen sink and break down various meats. Then he went to Truk, an island in Micronesia, to work at his uncle's wreck-diving resort, which attracted both Americans and Japanese. The visitors expected to eat well. It was there that he realized he loved working with food.

In Durham, Chris worked with Chef Ben Barker at Magnolia Grill for a couple of years, an experience that taught him much. "Ben opened my eyes to food and to doing things the proper way. I can never repay him for what he's taught me. He's basically given me my way of life," says Chris.

He then went to Nana's and worked for Chef Scott Howell, who at the time owned Pop's. Eventually, Scott sent Chris over to Pop's to work as a chef.

Meanwhile, after a time in France and at Colorado hotels, John ended up in Durham. He went to Nana's and also worked for Scott Howell, who sent him to Pop's. Chris was already working there.

The two joined in a partnership to buy Pop's from Scott. "We were just prepping one Saturday morning. Chris picked up the phone and called Scott and said, 'Hey, how much do you want?' " says John.

"Scott said an amount, and we scrounged around till we came up with it," says Chris. "At that time, we had a third partner, Matt Beason." Beason is now the owner of Six Plates Wine Bar. Chris and John "bought him out before we opened Rue Cler," says Chris. The camaraderie at Pop's infuses all who enter. The atmosphere is so lively and boisterous that people flock there all nights of the week. The menu changes regularly, depending on what comes in from the farmers and purveyors, but the staples—calamari and mussels—remain the same.

Much as at Rue Cler, "people come here to celebrate," says John.

"We see people eating and smiling and talking, having a good time. We can be a part of someone's life and never know it," says Chris. John remembers a man who came in for his first solid meal after heart surgery at Duke. He ordered mussels, and John took care of him the entire meal.

When farmers bring in their products—produce, fish, venison, chicken, lamb, pork, and eggs—in the morning, "we have no clue what's coming," says Chris. "It's an adventure every day." Whatever the bounty, the two restaurants share it.

"We're not going to get rich, but we're going to have fun," says Chris.

Writing about either Chris Stinnett or John Vandergrift without writing about the other would miss the point. The two are as closely bound as their restaurants. Half facetiously, Chris says, "We're married. I go to sleep thinking about the restaurants. He goes to sleep thinking about them." The difference between Pop's and Rue Cler is not as great as it seems at first. They're both neighborhood gathering places. Community places.

Chris and John share chef duties at the restaurants, spending six to eight months at a time in one or the other. The wait staff and some equipment are shared, too. Glasses, plates, and silverware move from one place to the other as needs arise.

Chef Chris says, "I'm a Southern boy." He grew up in Durham. "It's my Hotel California," he says. He loves the state and all its produce, which he finds similar to that of Italy and France. "How good we have it here," he says. "Durham is going to be the envy of the Triangle."

Outside dining at Pops with train in the background

Chef Chris Stinnett and Chef John Vandergrift's Pop's: A Durham Trattoria Recipes

POP'S POTATO GNOCCHI

Yields 60 gnocchi

3 Idaho potatoes
¼ cup Parmesan
Salt and pepper to taste
1 or 2 eggs
½ cup semolina flour
¾ cup all-purpose flour

Bake potatoes at 450 degrees for 1 hour or until soft. Cut slit in top of each potato to let steam escape. When potatoes are cool enough to work with but still warm, scrape out insides and run through a food mill or ricer or mash with a fork. Place potatoes in a mixing bowl. Add ingredients in the order listed above, mixing well after each addition. You must work with the dough quickly so starch does not get gummy and dough does not get too soft. Once dough comes together, turn it out onto a floured board and knead, working in about ¼ cup of additional flour to get a soft and slightly sticky consistency. You will need some extra semolina flour to roll dough out. If dough is too wet to work with, you can add some flour, but do not add too much or you will end up with gnocchi that tastes like flour, not potatoes.

Using ¼ of the dough at a time, roll out by hand into workable pieces that are ¾ to 1 inch in circumference. You should have 1 long "rope" of dough. Cut to desired size; Pop's cuts them to about 1 inch. Heat a pot of salted water to boiling as gnocchi dry for a few minutes. Place gnocchi in boiling water and cook for 2 to 3 minutes until they float. Remove from water with a slotted spoon, then place directly into your favorite sauce. Or you can brown them in butter or oil first in a sauté pan.

If you have extra gnocchi, you can freeze them raw. Spread them on a cookie sheet, dust with semolina, freeze, then bag for later use. Cooking time might be longer when using frozen gnocchi.

BALSAMIC VINAIGRETTE

Yields 2¼ cups

½ cup balsamic vinegar (use finest available)
½ teaspoon smooth Dijon mustard
½ shallot, minced
1½ cups olive oil (use finest available)
Salt and pepper to taste

Combine vinegar, mustard, and shallots. Whisk until thoroughly mixed. Slowly and steadily drip olive oil into vinegar mixture and whisk until emulsified—that is, until dressing thickens and turns glossy. Adjust seasonings. (Note: These steps can be performed in a blender; pour oil in a slow, steady stream until emulsified.) Mix with favorite greens and serve. Unused portion may be refrigerated for up to 1 week.

Amy Tornquist
at Watts Grocery

Watts Grocery
1116 Broad St.
Durham, N.C. 27705
919-416-5040
www.wattsgrocery.com

Directions

From Raleigh, take I-40 West to Exit 279B and follow N.C.
147 North (Durham Freeway) to Exit 14 (Swift Avenue/
Duke East Campus). Turn right at the light and continue
across Main Street onto Broad Street for four and a half
blocks to Watts Grocery, located on the right just before
West Club Boulevard. From Chapel Hill, take U.S. 15/501
Business (Durham–Chapel Hill Boulevard) to Exit 105B,
then follow U.S. 15/501 Bypass North to Exit 108B
(Durham Freeway South/N.C. 147). Go to Exit 14 (Swift
Avenue/Duke East Campus) and turn left at the light.
Continue past Main Street onto Broad Street for four and a
half blocks. Watts Grocery is on the right just before West
Club Boulevard.

Cuisine

This chef-owned restaurant serves North Carolina cuisine
made with French techniques and local ingredients.

Executive Chef Amy Tornquist grew up believing she could do
anything she wanted to do. After a summer with Bill Neal at Crook's
Corner in Chapel Hill (where Bill Smith is now chef), she knew she
wanted to be a chef. She pursued that goal with the same qualities that led
her to open Sage & Swift Gourmet Catering and now Watts Grocery—
namely, hard work and tenacity.

One summer when she was at the University of North Carolina at

Amy Tornquist

Chapel Hill, where she was an honors student who would graduate with two majors, she held a pair of jobs. One was an internship at the local newspaper *Independent Weekly*; the other was at Crook's Corner at night. She discovered that "being at Crook's was what I loved. It was the golden age then. Chef Bill Neal was still there directing the menu. Robert Stehling, who has recently won the James Beard Award for his Charleston, South Carolina, restaurant, Hominy Grill, was there. I worked with a wonderful kind of people. And the food was incredible," Amy says.

But an equally important factor was that Crook's "was an intellectually stimulating place to work. I like that a bunch. I liked the fact that I could have a trade and still be intellectually stimulated. I didn't have to have a job to seem smart. And that was before it was cool to be a chef," Amy says.

Since she is a French speaker, she went to France to attend Ecole de Cuisine La Varenne, where she worked with Anne Willan, Fernand Chambrette, and Claude Vauguet at the Parisian school. She did a stage at Duquesnoy, a Michelin Two Star restaurant in Paris, and later served as private chef at the British Embassy there. "France was great for a twenty-three to twenty-five-year-old," she says.

When she returned to Durham in 1992, though, she could not find a job that paid any more than she had made at Crook's a few years earlier. "So it seemed reasonable to open my own business. But I didn't want to open a restaurant at that time. I don't have a taste for risks," Amy says.

That was when she began Sage & Swift Gourmet Catering. The business was a success not only because of the gourmet food she served but also because she had grown up in Durham and had a large network of friends and family there.

Later, during a low period in the catering business, Amy worked again at Crook's Corner for six to eight months. While there, she met her future husband and business partner, artist and chef Jeremy Kerman. They now have two young children.

For about a year, she ran the Duke University Nasher Museum Café. Today, she continues to run Duke's Faculty Commons dining room, as well as Sage & Swift Gourmet Catering.

When she left Nasher, Amy decided she wanted to open her own restaurant. She called it Watts Grocery, after her old neighborhood store. After all, she believed she could do anything she wanted to do, with hard work and tenacity.

Watts Grocery interior with one of Jeremy Kerman's paintings

The restaurant has received rave reviews from national publications such as *Food & Wine, Bon Appétit, Condé Nast Traveler, Country Home,* and *Elegant Bride,* as well as from local press including the *Raleigh News & Observer,* the *Durham News,* Duke University's *Chronicle,* and *Raleigh Metro* magazine.

Her cuisine at Watts Grocery comes from the cooking she grew up with—her grandmother's. "I'm really all connected to North Carolina stuff. I spent a lot of time in eastern North Carolina small towns. They're really into seasons. They grow some produce, and a lot is bought locally." Every Saturday, Amy gets up at six to go to both the Durham and Carrboro farmers' markets.

The restaurant's design aims at giving it a homey feeling. Guests particularly enjoy the colors in Jeremy's paintings, which hang on all the walls. Sasha Berghausen with Ellen Cassilly Architects designed the interior, and Amy picked out the lights and fixtures. Flywheel Design did the logo.

But what makes the restaurant so popular is Chef Amy's North Carolina cuisine, inflected with French techniques and tastes, much like Bill Neal's.

Chef Amy Tornquist's Recipes

FARMER'S CHEESE HUSH PUPPIES

Makes about 30 hush puppies

2 cups plus 2½ tablespoons yellow stone-ground cornmeal
½ cup all-purpose flour
½ teaspoon baking soda
2 teaspoons baking powder
1 teaspoon salt
¼ cup sugar
½ cup chopped scallions
1½ cups buttermilk
½ cup butter, melted
½ pound farmer's cheese
1 egg
1 quart oil for frying

Mix dry ingredients in a large bowl. Add scallions, buttermilk, butter, cheese, and egg. Mix thoroughly. Pour oil into a fryer and heat to a simmer. Using a small ice-cream scoop, test for the correct temperature by dropping a scoop of mixture into oil. After about 1 minute, the outside should brown and the inside should be soft. Add scoops to oil until all mixture is used.

LAMB TAGINE WITH APRICOTS, OLIVES, AND BUTTERED ALMONDS

Serves 6

4 pounds bone-in lamb shoulder or neck or 2 to 4 pounds
    boneless lamb stew meat, cut into 2-inch chunks
4 cloves garlic, minced
½ teaspoon kosher salt

1 teaspoon black pepper
1 teaspoon sweet paprika
1 teaspoon ground ginger
¾ teaspoon ground cumin
2 large onions, peeled, quartered, and thinly sliced
3 cups water
2 2-inch cinnamon sticks
Large pinch saffron, crumbled
1¼ cups dried apricots, sliced, divided
1 cup cracked green olives, sliced from pits
2 to 4 tablespoons butter
⅓ cup sliced almonds
Cooked couscous
Chopped parsley or cilantro for garnish

Preheat oven to 325 degrees. Place meat in a deep Dutch oven or pot. Add garlic, salt, pepper, paprika, ginger, and cumin, rubbing spices over meat. Add ½ cup onions to lamb. Reserve additional onions. Cook meat over high heat for about 3 minutes; you do not have to brown it. Add water to pot, along with cinnamon and saffron. Bring to a simmer and cover pot. Transfer to oven and braise for 45 minutes. Take out of oven, turn meat, then top with remaining onion slices. Cover pot and braise for another 45 minutes until lamb is tender. Transfer meat to a bowl, leaving broth and onions in pot. Place pot on stove over high heat and add ¾ cup of the apricots and sliced olives. Simmer about 20 minutes until broth is reduced and thickened a bit. Return lamb to pot and keep warm.

To serve, chop remaining ½ cup apricot slices. Melt butter in a small skillet. Add almonds and cook about 2 minutes until browned and toasted. Serve lamb over couscous and top with almonds in butter and chopped apricots. Garnish with parsley or cilantro.

PECAN-PINEAPPLE POUND CAKE WITH RUM
Yields 2 9-inch round cakes, 2 tube pans, or 12 cupcakes

Pound Cake
2½ cups oil
4 cups sugar

6 eggs

1¼ cups fresh pineapple, finely chopped

½ cup sour cream

2 teaspoons Myers's rum

6 cups flour

2 teaspoons salt

2 teaspoons baking soda

3 cups North Carolina pecans, chopped

Preheat oven to 325 degrees. Prepare cake pans, tube pans, or cupcake holders with butter or oil. Cream oil and sugar. Add eggs 1 at a time and beat well after each addition. Add pineapple, sour cream, and rum. Blend until mixed. In a separate bowl, add flour, salt, and baking soda, blending well. Slowly add flour mixture ½ cup at a time to egg mixture, beating in each addition until thoroughly blended. Stir in pecans, mixing by hand. Pour into baking pans or cupcake holders. Bake for approximately 1 hour and 15 minutes until done. A tester should come out clean; sides of cake should be slightly away from pan.

Glaze

1 cup brown sugar

¾ cup butter

¾ cup cream

1 to 2 teaspoons rum

Mix all ingredients well. Spread glaze onto cakes or cupcakes.

John Vandergrift

John Vandergrift and Chris Stinnett
at Rue Cler

Rue Cler
401 East Chapel Hill St.
Durham, N.C. 27701
919-682-8844
john@ruecler-durham.com or chris@ruecler-durham.com
www.ruecler-durham.com

Directions

From Raleigh, take I-40 West to Exit 279B and go north on
Durham Freeway (N.C. 147) to Exit 14 (Swift Avenue/Duke
East Campus). Turn right at the light and go to the light at Main
Street. Turn right and continue about a mile to Five Points. Veer
left onto West Chapel Hill Street and continue to East Chapel
Hill Street. Rue Cler is on the left. Parking is available on the
street and in the garage across the street. From Chapel Hill, take
U.S. 15/501 Business (Durham–Chapel Hill Boulevard) to Exit
105A, then follow U.S. 15/501 Bypass to Exit 108A (Durham
Freeway South/N.C. 147). Go to Exit 14 (Swift Avenue/Duke
East Campus), turn left at the light, and go to the second light, at
Main Street. Turn right and continue about a mile to Five Points.
Veer left onto West Chapel Hill Street and continue to East
Chapel Hill Street. Rue Cler is on the left.

Cuisine

Rue Cler's two chefs own this French bistro–style restaurant.

The chefs at Pop's: A Durham Trattoria are the same as those at Rue
Cler. John Vandergrift and Chris Stinnett share time at each place. "We
will work fifteen days in a row, then take seven off. We're on a six- to

eight-month rotation at Rue Cler. The French restaurant gives us another outlet," says Chef Chris.

Chef John's experience in France was the motivating factor in creating Rue Cler. He grew up in Baltimore and started working in kitchens when he was fourteen. Then he had the chance to go to France when his father was transferred there. "I was really into food. I got the opportunity to work in kitchens over there several times over a three-year period," John says, "learning French techniques and cooking styles. In the winter, I worked at ski resorts in Colorado, ran banquets. I learned so much of the business end from it."

In 2001, he intended to go to New York after visiting a brother in North Carolina. They were at the beach when 9/11 happened. John changed his plans and moved to Durham.

A trattoria is very similar to a bistro. One is Italian and one is French. "A trattoria is more neighborhood-ish, though," says Chris. Both Rue Cler and Pop's have a family atmosphere where customers experience an informal welcome.

John and Chris want their customers to have fun at dinner. "At Rue Cler, we offer a thirty-dollar, three-course prix fixe menu," says John, "as well as the à la carte menu." Their menu features traditional bistro food— *steak frites*, coq au vin, and pâtés.

A bar and a television screen are in the restaurant. The unfinished walls give it a French Quarter atmosphere.

John and Chris share ownership of the two restaurants and the bakery that is part of Rue Cler. The bakery features espresso and the restaurant's own blend of coffee. In the morning before ten-thirty, locals stop by for coffee and beignets or crepes with the filling of the day. The bakery sells croissants and muffins for a quick breakfast. It also offers pizza dough and baguettes that customers can preorder to take home in the evening. The bakery is both a retail and a wholesale operation, selling to customers who walk in the door and also to many restaurants in the area.

Rue Cler was one of the first fine-dining restaurants to open in Durham's new gentrified downtown and has remained one of the favorites. "The food at Rue Cler is bistro style—simple and direct without the clutter of various components," says Chef Chris. The two chefs regard the restaurant as their creative outlet.

The bakery at Rue Cler

Chef John Vandergrift and Chef Chris Stinnett's Rue Cler Recipes

COQ AU VIN
Serves 4 to 6

Small bag of pearl onions
3- to 4-pound chicken, cut in pieces
1 cup flour
Salt and pepper to taste
3 tablespoons cooking oil
6 strips bacon, diced
4 stalks celery, diced to same size as pearl onions
3 carrots, diced to same size as pearl onions
4 cups red wine
3 cups chicken stock
2 to 3 sprigs fresh thyme
½ cup butter, softened

Peel pearl onions by cutting a small *x* in the root end of each. Pour boiling water over onions and soak for 2 minutes, then drain. Cut off root ends with a paring knife; the papery skin will peel right off. To save time, peel onions up to 2 days ahead, then chill.

Preheat oven to 400 degrees. Dust chicken with flour and add salt and pepper. In a braising pan or pot, heat oil over medium heat and brown chicken. Remove chicken, add bacon, and render until brown. Add pearl onions, celery, and carrots and brown in fat with bacon for 4 to 5 minutes. Deglaze with red wine and place chicken back in over vegetables. Bring to a boil and add chicken stock, thyme, and more salt and pepper. Bring to a boil again. Cover with foil and place in oven for 1½ hours. Remove from oven and check tenderness of chicken; if not tender, return to oven in 20-minute increments. Remove from oven, let rest 10 minutes, then remove chicken from pot. Add butter and stir to thicken. Adjust seasonings. Replace chicken and serve with crusty bread.

Interior of Rue Cler

GRATIN DAUPHINOISE (POTATO GRATIN)

Serves 4

3 Idaho russet potatoes, peeled
½ stick butter, room temperature
½ yellow onion, diced
Salt to taste
½ leek, outer leaves peeled off, split lengthwise, and washed
   thoroughly
1 cup dry white wine
2 cups heavy cream
Pepper to taste
1 cup shredded Gruyère cheese

Preheat oven to 350 degrees. Slice potatoes very thin with a Mandolin slicer. Cover with water to prevent browning. Use about 1 tablespoon of the butter to grease a 12-by-5-inch Pyrex baking dish. Melt remaining butter over medium heat in a 1-quart saucepan. Add onions and salt. While onions sweat, thinly slice leek. When onions are translucent, add leeks. Sweat onions and leeks until leeks wilt. Add wine. Boil 2 to 3 minutes, then add cream and pepper. Do not boil cream mixture. Once mixture reaches a simmer, remove from heat.

Drain potatoes and remove excess moisture with a paper towel. Arrange 1 layer of potatoes in bottom of pan, overlapping about ½ inch in a shingle-like pattern. Ladle enough cream mixture over potatoes to barely cover them when they are pressed slightly. Alternate sliced potatoes and cream mixture until ½ inch from top of dish. Barely cover potatoes with cream mixture. Spread cheese over top. Cover dish with plastic wrap and then aluminum foil and bake for 45 minutes, until potatoes in center offer just the slightest resistance to indicate doneness. Remove covers and finish cooking for about 15 minutes to brown cheese. Either serve hot with your favorite main course or chill for up to 4 days, cut into serving portions, and reheat in microwave or oven.

Raleigh

Sarig Agasi
PHOTO COURTESY ZELY & RITZ

Sarig Agasi
at Zely & Ritz

Zely & Ritz
301 Glenwood Ave.
Raleigh, N.C. 27603
919-828-0018
zelyandritz@gmail.com
www.zelyandritz.com
Directions
From Durham or Chapel Hill, take I-40 East to Exit
289. Follow Wade Avenue to Glenwood Avenue and
turn right. Go past Peace Street and continue for three
and a half blocks to the storefront Zely & Ritz, located
on the right behind a low hedge. Parking is in front.
Cuisine
This chef-owned restaurant serves Mediterranean and
Middle Eastern cuisine featuring fresh, organic, locally
grown products.

Chef Sarig Agasi grew up on a kibbutz (an Israeli agricultural community) eating an abundance of fresh in-season foods: avocados, mangoes, bananas, corn, tomatoes, figs, olives, passion fruit, lychees, papayas, cactus fruit, almonds, and pecans. He hunted wild boar and large porcupines and fished in the Mediterranean. "I had a fresh and green start from a very early age," he says. So it was only natural that he and Richard Holcomb became partners. But before that could happen, Sarig wended his way through South America, New York, and San Francisco before finally landing in Raleigh.

A citizen of Israel, Sarig joined the Israeli Air Force after graduating from high school, becoming part of an elite medical rescue unit. After meeting his wife, Nancy, on one of her trips from New York, the two traveled throughout South America, eating street food—"the most typical food," says Sarig. Then they went to New York City, where Nancy pursued her MBA at New York University while Sarig spent two years working in restaurants.

Sarig says, "I always liked to cook. My Polish grandmother, Zehava, was the one who gave me the inspiration all the time. So I made up my mind and said I didn't want to waste any more time." That was when he went to the California Culinary Academy at the age of twenty-nine. "I went to school to get the basics that I was missing," he says.

Back in New York after two years, Sarig worked with the chefs at Lespinasse for a year and a half and at Bouley's (the same restaurant where Scott Howell worked before going to Durham) for one year. By that time, Sarig and Nancy, busy with two of their eventual three children, began searching for a place where they could raise their family and open a successful restaurant. After reading an article in *Food & Wine* on Raleigh, they visited and made their decision to relocate there. Sarig began working in Durham at Scott Howell's Nana's. He stayed there for two and a half years.

"When we came to Raleigh, I always planned to open a restaurant," Sarig says. When the time came, he opened Butterflies, a high-end white-tablecloth restaurant in North Raleigh. Three things happened there: Butterflies got great reviews; Richard Holcomb, who had a software office nearby, discovered the place; and the North Raleigh clientele chose chain restaurants over Butterflies, which opened in 1999 and closed in 2003.

But an amazingly positive thing came out of that experience. Holcomb took special clients to Butterflies for dinner and knew the value of the restaurant. He told Sarig to come to him when he was ready to open another restaurant. Sarig already used fresh, local ingredients at Butterflies and planned to focus more on local farm products with his new restaurant, Zely & Ritz. Then Holcomb bought Coon Rock Farm in Hillsborough, and a partnership was born.

Sarig opened Zely & Ritz, named after his grandparents, in 2004. Holcomb bought the farm the next year. "At the time, it was really a no-brainer. I always liked to support local farmers, and after Richard purchased his farm I decided to, as much as possible, buy from Coon Rock Farm," Sarig says. What was unavailable at the farm he purchased "from around here—first in the state, then in Virginia and South Carolina," he says. "I

The bar at Zely & Ritz

want to get what I can from my state, including fish. I get prawns from the Mebane area. I get North Carolina shrimp, flounder, and snapper. Sometimes, I buy scallops from the North Sea and wild salmon from elsewhere. Lemons you can't get here. Olives and olive oil you can't get here. But I try to keep it all in the American market first."

Sarig says, "It came to a point that I said, 'I really want to focus on who I am.' Now, we have a restaurant-farm partnership. We get eggs, meat, produce from the farm. Our waste from the table and kitchen goes back to the farm to feed our chickens, hogs, and vegetables. This is a big difference between Zely & Ritz and other restaurants in the Triangle."

The cuisine at Zely & Ritz is Mediterranean and Middle Eastern, prepared using French techniques and absolutely fresh local ingredients. A second restaurant from the same corporation that owns Zely & Ritz will open in Durham in the fall of 2009. Eno Restaurant, to be located at 102 City Hall Plaza, will feature Southern cuisine. The corporation will welcome a fourth member, expanding from Sarig, Nancy, and Richard Holcomb to include Jamie DeMent. Sarig will be the executive chef of both restaurants.

Though customers can buy produce at Zely & Ritz, Eno will have an attached market to sell the farm's products. It will do well, Sarig says, because "Durham is a place where there are people who care about what they eat."

Zely & Ritz, as the name implies, is a family affair. Nancy takes care of the wine selections and managerial duties. The couple's oldest son is now host on Saturday nights. At Eno, Executive Chef Sarig will cook and oversee the menu, Nancy will provide the wine selections, and Holcomb and DeMent will manage the farm from which the bounty comes.

Chef Sarig Agasi's Recipes

ROASTED COON ROCK FARM CHICKEN BREAST WITH GRILLED EGGPLANT, BRAISED BABY BOK CHOY, AND HONEY-GINGER SAUCE

Serves 2

Extra-virgin olive oil
Pinch of organic unsalted butter
Salt and pepper to taste
1 boneless organic free-range chicken breast with skin
1 small organic eggplant, halved
1 baby organic bok choy
¼ cup honey, divided
1 tablespoon grated fresh ginger
¼ cup chicken stock or broth
1 tablespoon mixed organic fresh herbs (parsley, thyme, marjoram, and sage), chopped
Fresh ginger, peeled and thinly sliced

Preheat oven to 350 degrees. Heat olive oil and butter in an ovenproof skillet or sauté pan over medium-high heat. Salt and pepper chicken breast. Sauté chicken with skin side down for about 5 minutes until skin is a crispy golden brown. Flip chicken over and put pan in oven for 10 minutes. Meanwhile, preheat a grill or grill pan and brush with olive oil. Drizzle eggplant with olive oil, add salt and pepper, and grill on each cut side for 5 minutes. Remove eggplant from heat. Cut baby bok choy lengthwise and wash well. Remove chicken from oven and set aside to rest. In the same pan, add eggplant and bok choy. Pour half of honey into pan over vegetables and cook over low heat until honey bubbles. Add ginger, chicken stock or broth, and mixed herbs. Cover pan and cook over low heat for about 5 minutes. Remove cover. Cut chicken breast in half on the bias and put back in pan with vegetables and liquid to finish cooking. Add remaining honey so chicken breast is nicely golden.

To plate, garnish with ginger.

BEET, PEAR, FETA CHEESE, AND WALNUT SALAD

Serves 4

Salad

1 bunch fresh beets (can use more than one variety, if desired)
Light olive oil
Salt and freshly ground pepper to taste
½ cup walnuts
2 D'Anjou pears, peeled and cored
¼ pound feta cheese
1 pound organic mixed greens

Preheat oven to 400 degrees. Cut off leaves and wash beets in cold water. Place beets in a roasting pan and drizzle with olive oil (do not use extra-virgin oil because it will smoke). Sprinkle with salt and pepper. Cover pan with foil and roast in oven for about 1 hour until beets are soft. Remove from oven and cool to a comfortable temperature, then peel and dice beets into ½-inch cubes. Save beet juice from roasting pan.

Reduce oven to 350 degrees. Toast walnuts on a sheet pan in oven for about 15 minutes. Cut pears into ½-inch cubes. Cube feta cheese to the same size. Set aside beets, walnuts, pears, feta, and mixed greens.

Walnut Vinaigrette

Yields 1½ cups

1 shallot, finely chopped
¼ cup walnut oil
¼ cup red wine vinegar
1 tablespoon balsamic vinegar
1 tablespoon honey
½ cup water
Juice from roasted beets
Salt and freshly ground pepper to taste

In a stainless-steel bowl, whisk shallots with walnut oil, red wine vinegar, balsamic vinegar, and honey. Whisk in water and beet juice. Add salt and pepper. Vinaigrette may be refrigerated for up to 3 days.

To assemble, put mixed greens into a large stainless-steel bowl. Add beets, walnuts, pears, and feta. Add about ⅛ cup vinaigrette for each serving and toss.

Ashley Christensen
at Poole's Downtown Diner

Poole's Downtown Diner
426 South McDowell St.
Raleigh, N.C. 27601
919-832-4477
www.poolesdowntowndiner.com
Directions
From Durham or Chapel Hill, take I-40 East to
Exit 289. Follow Wade Avenue to St. Mary's Street,
turn right, go to Hillsborough Street, and turn left.
Go to North Dawson Street, turn right, go to West
Cabarrus Street, turn left, go one block to South
McDowell Street, and turn left. Poole's Downtown
Diner is on the left after half a block. Parking is
on the street. Poole's is diagonally across from the
Raleigh Civic and Convention Center.
Cuisine
This chef-owned restaurant serves seasonal New
American Cuisine with Southern influences.

Executive Chef Ashley Christensen purchased a landmark restaurant
in 2007 and is preserving not only the ambience of the place but also the
"innate beginnings of a dish so they are clear in the final product." The care
and love she has for Poole's Downtown Diner show in the way she treats
the guests at the former 1940s pie shop and luncheonette.

Born in Greensboro, Ashley grew up in Kernersville. She went to
Raleigh as a student when she was eighteen, beginning her cooking career
by catering dinners at North Carolina State University. Her connection
to Poole's started when her father visited her in Raleigh, saw the diner,

Ashley Christensen

and told her he had eaten there daily when he was nineteen. The diner was built in 1947. Even with essential upgrades, it looks the same as it did then. The picture of Poole's on the website shows a young girl sitting at the counter. She is now the seventy-six-year-old owner of the building.

Ashley's earliest influence was Chef Andrea Reusing, who was at Enoteca Vin at the time. Ashley worked with her for about a year. "Through her, I was exposed to a lot of great ingredients and the sources of those ingredients. Being a young cook, I wasn't familiar with how to get in touch with those folks, the providers. She definitely is extremely inspiring to me. Andrea is amazing for someone who was self-taught. I just watched her and picked up on her sense of classic techniques. She is brilliant and accomplished," says Ashley.

Her next experience was with Chef Scott Howell—"a fantastic teacher," says Ashley. "Everything I wanted to know while I was there, he made a great effort to teach me. He strives to share his knowledge, and he is a significant contributor to my career. I had engaging conversations with him. He'd show me a technique and then say, 'Okay, go ahead.'" She adds, "He's one of a kind."

Ashley was executive chef at the now-defunct Enoteca Vin in Raleigh for seven years. After she bought Poole's, she remained in that capacity, doing two jobs until she left to work at Poole's full-time in 2008.

Ashley's goal with Poole's is "to enjoy it. To practice something every day that I love and enjoy." She offers "straightforward, honest, enjoyable food," she says. "We take care of guests and offer something that is honest. We teach people about value, not bargain. This restaurant is a great value."

The formula must be working, since Poole's has many regular patrons, including musicians, dancers, and other entertainers who come in from the Raleigh Civic and Convention Center across the street. "I want people to call this place their own," Ashley says. "Not a day goes by that we don't say thank you for that."

Ashley characterizes herself as a perfectionist. "I work hard every day to get better and better at what I do. We don't ever compromise." She describes the hundreds of tasting spoons in the kitchen, used to sample the food before it goes out to guests. "I cook because it drives me crazy not to be on line. I will never design a kitchen where I can't see everything."

A people person, Ashley learned about entertaining from her parents, and it shows at Poole's. Her parents gave dinner parties featuring good food, good music, and good wine. "It wasn't just about nutrition," she says. "And I do enjoy the social aspect of the restaurant."

She interacts with guests as much as she can. "I pop out and say hello. We have the most amazing conversations. People come in and tell us stories about this place."

She gives careful attention to the details of the food offered to guests—to its production, its design, its presentation, the whole experience. "The process is thoughtful," says Chef Ashley. "The cuisine is simple. It is important to be able to taste the beginnings of a dish." She uses fresh local ingredients and is on the board of the new Moore Square Farmers Market, located down the street from Poole's. "It's Raleigh's first downtown hand-selling market with a heavy focus on organic."

Executive Chef Ashley Christensen's Recipes

MACARONI AU GRATIN
Serves 4 to 6

3 cups heavy cream
1 cup shredded Gruyère cheese, divided
1 cup shredded Asiago cheese, divided
1 cup shredded white cheddar cheese, divided
½ pound macaroni, cooked al dente and drained
2 tablespoons cold butter
Pinch of sea salt
Cracked black pepper to taste

Set a rack in the oven about 4 inches from broiler. Preheat broiler. If broiler has settings, use a low-temperature option. Butter an 8-by-10-inch ovenproof dish. In a very large sauté pan over medium-high heat, reduce cream by ¼. Lower heat to medium. Add ¾ cup each of Gruyère, Asiago, and white cheddar and stir until cheeses are melted. Add macaroni. Stir with a wooden spoon, tossing contents. Add butter and salt and continue stirring until butter is emulsified (melted and integrated) into sauce. Transfer mixture to baking dish. (If you wish to add extra ingredients such as roasted tomatoes or caramelized onions, they should be layered between the pasta and the cheese topping at this point.) Sprinkle remaining ¼ cup each of Gruyère, Asiago, and white cheddar over top, distributing evenly. Place dish under broiler. Watch carefully, as you will need to rotate dish to create an even crust. This will take 3 to 5 minutes or longer, depending on strength of broiler. Remove gratin from oven and season with pepper. Serve immediately.

Poole's historic counter

BOURBON CHOCOLATE HAZELNUT PIE

Serves 8 to 10

Crust

1½ cups sifted all-purpose flour
1 teaspoon salt
1 stick butter, cut into small pieces and chilled
3 tablespoons ice water

Preheat oven to 350 degrees. Grease a deep 9-inch pie dish. Combine flour and salt in a mixing bowl. Using a pastry blender or 2 forks, cut butter into flour mixture. The mixture should have a course, sandy texture with some pea-sized butter pieces. Mix in just enough ice water so that dough forms into a ball. Do not knead dough, but work it just enough to form ball. Flatten dough and wrap in plastic. Allow to rest in refrigerator at least 2 hours until thoroughly chilled.

Place dough on a floured surface and roll to ⅛-inch thickness. Line pie dish with dough and trim edges. Prick bottom of crust with a fork, fill with pie weights (dried beans or rice will work), and bake about 18 minutes, rotating halfway through, until edges are golden brown. Remove from oven, remove pie weights, and set aside.

Filling

5 eggs
1 cup sugar
½ cup brown sugar
1 teaspoon salt
6 tablespoons melted butter
1 teaspoon vanilla
¼ cup bourbon, or to taste (Poole's uses Basil Hayden's bourbon)
1½ cups hazelnut pieces
1 cup dark chocolate chips (70 percent cacao)

Preheat oven to 350 degrees. Beat eggs with sugar, brown sugar, salt, butter, vanilla, and bourbon, mixing until thoroughly combined. Layer hazelnut pieces and chocolate chips in bottom of pastry shell. Carefully pour filling over hazelnuts and chocolate chips. Bake until filling is set and edges are firm. The center will still be slightly jiggly. Check pie after 30 minutes and every 5 minutes afterward until done. Allow to cool completely before serving.

Walter Royal
at Angus Barn

Angus Barn
9401 Glenwood Ave. (U.S. 70 at Aviation Pkwy.)
Raleigh, N.C. 27617
919-781-2444
www.angusbarn.com
Directions
From Raleigh, take Glenwood Avenue North to Angus
Barn, on the left. From Durham or Chapel Hill, take
I-40 East and exit onto I-540. Continue to Exit 4A
(U.S. 70/Glenwood Avenue). Go south through the
stoplight to Angus Barn, located up the hill on the right.
Cuisine
This restaurant specializes in corn-fed Midwestern beef
and serves a wide range of meat and seafood entrées.

You would not think a man as tall and imposing and accomplished as Chef Walter Royal would be unassuming. But he is. This cool Iron Chef, winner of a competition with Chef Cat Cora, oversees the feeding of more than 240,000 customers a year. Angus Barn, built to look like a big red barn, is one of the Triangle's, if not the country's, finest restaurants.

Walter was born in rural Eclectic, Alabama, not too far from Montgomery. He says, "Part of my DNA is food. I used to visit my grandmother in Cottage Grove, really rural, and I loved going down there. Figs, peaches, blackberries. We would go down by the river. Watercress,

Walter Royal

wild asparagus. These were things I was privy to as a child, and most people have no clue about them. My grandparents had hogs and chickens and cows and goats. We always had a freezer full of meat."

But, says Walter, "the person who most inspired me to be a cook was my aunt Vertal. Her tea cookies. They would just dissolve in your mouth. I was four. They made me want to take something as simple as flour, butter, and sugar and make something so wonderful."

Because his parents, mill workers, wanted their children to have a better life, Walter left rural Alabama to attend college on a football scholarship. He also worked in restaurants to earn money. After earning a degree in psychology, he worked in the mental health field, helping mentally handicapped individuals adjust to the normal world. But he always worked in restaurants.

One day, he admitted his fascination with food and auditioned for a class with cookbook author Nathalie Dupree in Rich's Department Store in Atlanta, Georgia. "She liked what I did, and she's been a friend ever since," he says. He took her course. Afterward, she made a phone call to Jenny and R. B. Fitch, the developers of Fearrington Village in Pittsboro—the same Fitches who discovered Chef Bill Neal, Chef Ben Barker, and Pastry Chef Karen Barker. The Fitches took Walter to meet their chef at that time, Edna Lewis, the legendary Southern chef who introduced Southern cuisine to New Yorkers.

"Meeting with Edna was just like the sun coming through the clouds," he says. "Edna was methodical and very to-the-point and passionate about Southern cuisine. She wanted the best, and she demanded the best from everyone. She encouraged me to stick with what I knew, what I believed in, and said, 'It will pay off.' "

That philosophy led him to the Food Network's *Iron Chef* show in 2006. "I know everybody thinks Californian and French cuisines are the best, but I'm a Southern boy through and through. Look at Bill Neal. Southern cuisine. Look at Ben Barker. He rode in on the wagon and does good, elegant Southern cuisine. And he threw in his training from the CIA [Culinary Institute of America]," Walter says.

After working with Chef Edna Lewis, Walter became *sous chef* at Magnolia Grill with Chef Ben Barker. "Ben and I were, and are, great friends," Walter says. Following five years working with the mentally handicapped and five years each with Edna Lewis and Ben Barker, he had developed his own philosophy of life and of working in the kitchen. "I'm never going to stand on the rooftop and say, 'I did this. I did that.' It's not my style. I give you the tools to get to the next level. I ask nothing more than for you to pass it on. It costs very little to give a person a glass of water if they're thirsty, encouragement when they're down," he says. "That's what life should be about."

Walter's life experiences prepared him for the gargantuan task of becoming executive chef at Angus Barn, one of the country's busiest restaurants. Van Eure now operates the restaurant that was established by her parents, Thad and Alice Eure. Walter was thirty-seven years old in September 1996 when he joined Angus Barn. "They knew I wasn't spotlight-hungry. They knew I could be taught the Angus Barn style," he says. "Was I scared to death? I worked night and day, seven days a week."

As executive chef at Angus Barn, Walter makes sixteen trips a year to give talks, conduct demonstrations, and teach classes in places like Savannah, Georgia; Charleston, South Carolina; and Snowshoe, West Virginia. He also visits one international site each year. For the past ten years, he and the restaurant have mentored young people who show promise for working in the food industry. One of them, Chris Thanhouser, was twelve years old at the time he assisted Walter in the *Iron Chef* competition. Chris is the son of Van Eure and a likely candidate for future executive chef.

When Walter was chosen to be a contestant on the live Food Network program, he was given the right to choose his competitor from the 2006 season's chefs. He chose Cat Cora because she is a Southern chef. But on the show, they were given ostrich and instructed to prepare a dinner in one hour. Walter went "in my zone." As Edna Lewis had advised him years earlier, "I stuck with the basics. I stuck with what I know." Out of the ostrich egg, he made Edna's chocolate soufflé. "It's my go-to dessert. That and lemon bars." The end result of his being true to himself was that he won the *Iron Chef* competition with the help of his *sous chefs*, Julia Strickland, Alan McSwain, and young Chris Thanhouser.

Angus Barn has two new dining rooms—the Alice Wine Cellar and the Thad Wine Cellar. There, Chef Walter oversees gourmet dinners paired with wines from *Wine Spectator*'s Grand Award wine collection and serves as chef when asked to do so. Soon, he will begin a cookbook. "I've been saving recipes for years," he says.

Interior of Angus Barn

Executive Chef Walter Royal's Recipes

CHOCOLATE SOUFFLÉ WITH FUDGE SAUCE

Serves 6 to 8

Fudge Sauce

Makes 1½ cups
¾ cup sugar
3 tablespoons unsweetened chocolate, chopped
1⅔ cups evaporated milk
1 teaspoon vanilla

In a medium saucepan, stir together sugar and chocolate. Add evaporated milk and stir to blend. Bring to a full rolling boil, stirring constantly. Boil 8 to 10 minutes. Remove from heat and stir in vanilla. Serve warm or cool.

Soufflé

½ cup flour
1¾ cups sugar, divided
1½ cups milk
3 squares unsweetened chocolate, coarsely chopped or grated
6 eggs, separated
Butter for greasing soufflé dish
2 teaspoons vanilla
Powdered sugar for dusting

About 2 hours before serving, mix flour and 1½ cups of the sugar in a 2-quart saucepan, using a wire whisk. Slowly stir in milk until smooth. Cook over medium heat, stirring constantly, until mixture thickens and boils. Cook 1 additional minute and remove from heat. Stir chocolate pieces into mixture until melted. Temper egg yolks by adding a small amount of hot mixture to yolks to gradually raise their temperature. Then very slowly add yolks to chocolate mixture, mixing well. Refrigerate until cool to lukewarm. Stir occasionally.

Preheat oven to 375 degrees. Grease a 2½-quart soufflé dish with butter and sprinkle with a small amount of sugar. In a large bowl, beat egg whites with mixer at high speed until soft peaks form. Sprinkle in remaining ¼ cup sugar and continue to beat until sugar is completely dissolved. Whites should stand stiff. Fold in cooled chocolate mixture ⅓ at a time. Add vanilla and mix. Pour mixture into soufflé dish, leaving 1 inch from the top for expansion. Bake 35 to 40 minutes until a knife inserted in mixture comes out clean.

When soufflé is done, sprinkle with powdered sugar. Serve immediately, topped with fudge sauce.

LEMON BARS
Yields 36 bars

2 cups plus 3 tablespoons all-purpose flour, divided
½ cup powdered sugar
2 tablespoons cornstarch
½ teaspoon salt
¾ cup butter
4 eggs, lightly beaten
1½ cups sugar
1 teaspoon lemon zest, finely grated
¾ to 1 cup fresh lemon juice
¼ cup half-and-half, light cream, or whole milk
Powdered sugar for dusting

Preheat oven to 350 degrees. Line a 13-by-9-by-2-inch baking pan with aluminum foil, leaving a 1- to 2-inch overhang. Grease the foil and set aside. In a large bowl, combine 2 cups of the flour, powdered sugar, cornstarch, and salt. Using a pastry blender, cut in butter until mixture resembles coarse crumbs. Press mixture into bottom of prepared pan. Bake for 18 to 20 minutes until edges are golden. Remove from oven.

Meanwhile, in a medium bowl, whisk together eggs, sugar, remaining 3 tablespoons of flour, lemon zest, lemon juice, and half-and-half. Pour filling over hot crust. Bake for 15 to 20 minutes more until center is set. Remove from oven and cool completely. Grasp foil overhang and lift from pan. Cut into bars. Right before serving, sift powdered sugar over bars.

Daniel Schurr

Daniel Schurr
at Second Empire Restaurant and Tavern

Second Empire Restaurant and Tavern
330 Hillsborough St.
Raleigh, N.C. 27603
919-829-3663
www.second-empire.com
Directions
From Durham or Chapel Hill, take I-40 East to Exit
289 and follow Wade Avenue to St. Mary's Street. Turn
right, go to Hillsborough Street, and turn left. Second
Empire is on the left.
Cuisine
This restaurant serves New American cuisine with
French influences, using fresh seasonal ingredients.

Executive Chef Daniel Schurr does not use a cookbook. Everything he needs is in his head and heart. He has been cooking since he dropped out of Greensboro College, where he took classes in philosophy and history and avoided math. Then his father took his credit cards away, saying, "Son, you'd better learn how to do something because you've got expensive tastes. And you'd better be good at it." Though he had already been introduced to the food world, he then decided to devote himself to it.

Born in Miami, Daniel came with his family to North Carolina in 1977, when he was in the seventh grade. He often dined in white-tablecloth restaurants with his father and grandfather. Later, his father took the family to superior hotels and the best restaurants when they traveled. His grandmother in the town of Liberty, North Carolina, also greatly influenced him. She was the kind of cook who knew how to make sourdough starter and fried pies.

When Daniel did as his father told him, his first job was as back-boy in the Holiday Inn on I-40 in Greensboro. He worked in the bar putting ice into glasses and cutting lemons.

Quickly, though, he began working with the chef, a practitioner of Nouvelle Cuisine who had been brought in from California. "I worked my way up real fast," says Daniel, "and he sent me on to the chef-owned Equinox Restaurant and Bakery in Greensboro, a happening spot. There was a bakery and catering, and they served breakfast, lunch, and dinner." He was introduced to very hard work.

"I got really involved with cooking there," he says. The chef at Equinox encouraged Daniel to go to the Culinary Institute of America. There, the college dropout finished first in his class and was voted most likely to succeed.

His most important experience after graduating from the Culinary Institute was his tenure with his mentor, Chef Jean Marie Lacroix of the Fountain Dining Room in the Four Seasons Hotel in Philadelphia. He stayed with Chef Lacroix for seven and a half years, thoroughly learning the true techniques of French cooking. At the Four Seasons, "I learned so much, saw so much. I participated in every aspect of what a chef could do, even though I was still focused on cooking. I wasn't thinking of becoming a chef," Daniel says.

However, after so many years away from home, it was time to return. But instead of heading to Liberty or Greensboro, he chose Raleigh, accepting the position of executive chef at Angus Barn—the position now held by Walter Royal. He was there just ten months before an opportunity arose that would change his life: a restaurant in a house in the midst of busy Raleigh.

It so happened that attorney and developer Ted Reynolds, his wife, and his daughter Kim had bought from Angus Barn's owner, the late Alice Eure, an old house on Hillsborough Street a few blocks from the State Capitol. It was known as the Dodd-Hinsdale House, the last of the Second Empire Victorian houses that once lined the street. After Reynolds made the decision to save the house, he and his daughter resolved to restore it and open a restaurant. All they needed was an outstanding chef to match the glory of the house.

Second Empire interior

Charlie Winston, cofounder of Angus Barn, hotelier, and a man well known in Raleigh, had met Daniel at Angus Barn and knew that Reynolds was looking for a chef. So Daniel and Reynolds talked and agreed that he would become chef and part owner. "It took two years to restore the house, and now the restaurant has been open since 1997. Reynolds's whole intent was to save the house for Raleigh," says Daniel.

Daniel did not aspire to be a chef. He was fulfilled as a cook. "It takes at least ten years to be a good cook. You need the repetition to learn the methods. You have to do things over and over." Now, he is executive chef at Second Empire Restaurant and Tavern. The difference between being a cook and a chef, he says, is that "a chef manages, assures quality, puts out the finest product, and still cooks. A chef is a leader. A chef is willing to teach and give back. A chef is an inspiration." A chef creates a good team. "To put out good food takes a good team," he says.

Daniel's kitchen in Second Empire reflects his philosophy. It is shiny-clean, predominantly white and stainless steel, with inspirational sayings on the walls such as, "Ability can take you to the top, but it takes character to keep you there." The size of a one-bedroom, one-bath house, the kitchen hums along with the usual clanging and banging.

His cuisine is based on French techniques and American influences.

The staircase at Second Empire Restaurant and Tavern

"Reduction sauces, stocks, no seeds, no skins. Everything is about the palate, how it feels in the mouth," he says. "Presentation is very important to me. You taste with your eyes. Make sure it looks good as well as tastes good."

His focus centers on the plate. "Everything else is in the background. Crunch or purée. Acid or sweet. Everything balances. And always use the freshest, best product. When you bite into something, you'll get a sensation of all the flavors on the plate," he says.

He has a natural ability "to understand the way things feel and look, a natural chemistry," he says. Given his talent and long experience, he does not need or use cookbooks.

"I love what I do," Chef Daniel says. "I enjoy it." As a result, he wants to give back to the city that has been so good to him. He prepares food for the Church of the Good Shepherd Soup Kitchen for the homeless, while Kim Reynolds and Second Empire sponsor a 5K run to benefit Camp Woodbine for hearing-impaired children.

Executive Chef Daniel Schurr's Recipes

BRAISED SPRING LAMB SHANK WITH CREAMY POLENTA AND DRIED DATES, SWISS CHARD, ROASTED ROOT VEGETABLES, AND NATURAL JUS

Serves 4 to 6

Braised Lamb Shank
1 pound (2 pieces) French-trimmed* lamb shank
Salt and pepper to taste
3 tablespoons olive oil
½ cup chopped onions
½ cup chopped carrots
½ cup chopped celery
2 cloves garlic, chopped
1 sprig thyme
1 bay leaf
1 tablespoon black peppercorns
¼ cup tomato paste

Preheat oven to 350 degrees. Season lamb generously with salt and pepper and sear in olive oil in an earthenware pot.

Let lamb brown on all sides to seal in flavor. In same pot, add onions, carrots, celery, garlic, thyme, bay leaf, and peppercorns and let brown in fat until caramelized. Add tomato paste and caramelize. Add cold water to cover lamb. Put lid on pot and bake in oven about 2½ hours until fork tender. Strain braising liquid. In a saucepot, simmer strained liquid until reduced by half. The sauce may be served over polenta.

* You can buy lamb shanks French-trimmed. French-trimmed is when all meat and fat are removed from 1 end of a bone.

Roasted Root Vegetables

1 turnip
1 rutabaga
1 parsnip
1 carrot
2 tablespoons olive oil
Salt and pepper to taste

Preheat oven to 375 degrees. Peel and dice vegetables. Place vegetables in a baking pan, lightly coat in olive oil, and toss. Season with salt and pepper. Roast vegetables in oven for approximately 45 minutes until lightly caramelized and tender.

Polenta

1 cup water
⅓ cup quick-cooking polenta (use high-quality Express corn polenta or regular polenta)
¼ cup shredded Fontina cheese
¼ cup dried dates, chopped
Salt and pepper to taste

Bring water to a boil. Whisk in polenta until it comes together like hot cereal. Simmer on low heat for 3 to 5 minutes (longer with regular polenta), stirring constantly. Fold in cheese and dates. Season with salt and pepper. Scrape cooked polenta into a greased stainless-steel bowl. When firm, upend onto a serving platter or cutting board and slice for serving.

Braised Swiss Chard

1 tablespoon butter
⅛ cup minced fresh ginger
⅛ cup minced shallots
⅛ cup minced garlic
4 ribs Swiss chard, stems removed, leaves only, cleaned and
    rinsed
Salt and pepper to taste
½ cup chicken broth

Melt butter. Add ginger, shallots, and garlic and sauté until translucent and no longer crunchy. Add Swiss chard leaves. Add salt and pepper. Add chicken broth. Cover and cook about 5 to 7 minutes until tender.

·····················

To plate, place lamb on plates with roasted root vegetables, Swiss chard, and polenta. Serve sauce over polenta and lamb.

SWEET POTATO BREAD PUDDING

Serves 13

Sweet Potato Purée

3 large sweet potatoes, peeled
1 tablespoon olive oil
Salt and pepper to taste

Preheat oven to 375 degrees. Coat sweet potatoes with olive oil. Lightly salt and pepper. Place potatoes in a baking pan and bake for 1 hour until soft. When cooled, purée in a food processor. Set aside.

Bread Pudding

1 cup dried cherries
¼ cup dried cranberries
1 cup whole milk
1 quart heavy cream
1¼ cups brown sugar
4 eggs plus 1 egg yolk

1 large, dense, heavy loaf of bread, diced
1½ to 2 teaspoons cinnamon
½ teaspoon nutmeg
Panko breadcrumbs as needed

Preheat oven to 350 degrees. Cover cherries and cranberries with water and soak until plump. Drain. Heat milk, cream, and sugar, stirring until sugar is dissolved. Bring to a light boil. Remove from heat but keep warm. Temper eggs and yolk by whisking in small amounts of heated milk and cream mixture until egg mixture is warmed. Gradually add tempered egg mixture to milk and cream mixture, whisking the entire time. Place diced bread in a large mixing bowl. Pour hot liquid over bread and stir to coat. Add cinnamon, nutmeg, sweet potato purée, cherries, and cranberries. Fold just until combined. Cover with foil and let soak 10 minutes. Stir and let soak covered 10 more minutes. Butter thirteen 8-ounce ramekins and lightly coat with panko crumbs. Fill ramekins ¾ full. Bake about 30 minutes until set.

Jason Smith
at 18 Seaboard

18 Seaboard
18 Seaboard Ave., Suite 100
Raleigh, N.C. 27604
919-861-4318
jsmith@18seaboard.com
www.18seaboard.com
Directions
From Durham or Chapel Hill, take I-40 East to Exit
289, follow Wade Avenue to Glenwood Avenue,
and turn right. Go to West Peace Street, turn left, go
to Halifax Street, turn left, and go to West Franklin
Street (Seaboard Avenue). The first building on the
left houses 18 Seaboard.
Cuisine
This chef-owned restaurant serves seasonal,
contemporary comfort food.

Chef Jason Smith was born in Raleigh. After moving to Wilmington, New York City, and Antarctica, he came back home. Along the way, he learned that he most wanted to make people happy. And he is doing just that in his restaurant, 18 Seaboard.

Jason's earliest experiences with food were with his grandmothers, who were "serious Southern cooks. When we were eating lunch, we were talking about what we were cooking for dinner. When we were eating

Jason Smith

dinner, we were talking about what we were going to eat for breakfast the next morning." And for Christmas, "my grandmother was talking about what we were going to have at Christmas dinner a year later."

Jason began cooking for himself when he got home from school because his parents worked. Through that experience, "I became intrigued with food and how to prepare it," he says.

Deciding not to go to culinary school, Jason worked for Chef Ben Barker and Pastry Chef Karen Barker at Magnolia Grill for two and a half years. "The greatest influence on my cuisine was Ben and Karen Barker. I saw the relationship they had with purveyors. I saw their creative cuisine," he says. "They've done a great service for the entire Southeast."

It was at Magnolia Grill that he fell in love with food, but it was in New York that he fell in love with the restaurant business. Chef Danny Meyer, whose restaurants include Gramercy Tavern and Union Square Café, "showed me how hospitality is worked into the business and how to manage the money part," says Jason.

Then came 9/11, and Jason decided to leave New York. At the age of thirty, he found work as a chef for the National Science Foundation at McMurdo Station on Ross Island in Antarctica. He cooked breakfast and lunch cafeteria-style for fourteen hundred support staff and scientists. "It was a very rewarding experience," he says. "I learned so much, including leadership skills. There was great scenery, and there were great folks."

He put all those attributes together—love of food, knowledge of the restaurant business, and leadership skills—and opened his own restaurant in the same area of downtown Raleigh where his grandfathers had worked and his father now works. "Now, we've had three generations in downtown Raleigh," says Jason. He decided on a cooking career for several reasons: "One, I love people. In this restaurant, I can interact with three hundred people a day. Two, there is the creativity of cooking, finding new ingredients, new techniques. Three, I love the adrenaline, the rush. And four, at the end of the day, there's some money in the bank."

The restaurant business, says Jason, "is in the details, in the atmosphere, the sights, the smells, the lighting—the whole experience. And I love all those details. I want to make people feel as good as I do when I go out."

Jason says he is not a perfectionist. "I just want to do the best we're able to do. It's hard for things to be perfect when 150 people show up at seven o'clock." (His restaurant has 120 seatings a night.) Rather, his goal is for guests to have an outstanding experience in enjoying good food at a

Interior of 18 Seaboard

reasonable price. "I want to be the busiest chef in the Triangle," he says. "I want people to be comfortable and to enjoy the experience of being here. I want to make people feel warm and welcome. We have the opportunity for two hours to take the guests' minds off their worries. I do the best job I can."

Just as important as creating a comfortable, welcoming environment is Jason's emphasis on fine food. The restaurant prints menus every two or three days to reflect seasonal products. North Carolina fish is one of the primary items. "All seafood is local except scallops and salmon," he says. For example, 18 Seaboard offers she-crab soup made every night from live blue crabs. One variation is Carolina Coast She-Crab Soup with Sweet Sherry Reduction. At the peak of summer, Jason uses "a lot of local products."

Chef Jason has a wife and a baby daughter. He is in the process of opening a second restaurant in the area. "This is not a hobby," he says. "This is how I make my living."

Chef Jason Smith's Recipes

CHAMPAGNE TARRAGON BUTTER

"This sauce complements all types of seafood selections wonderfully. Many of our dishes spend time on our wood-fired grill, and this sauce helps to add a little sophistication to the smoky flavor that so many people enjoy," Chef Jason says.

Yields 1 cup

6 peppercorns
2 tablespoons fresh tarragon
1 shallot, sliced
1 cup dry sparkling wine
1 pound unsalted butter
Salt to taste

In a small saucepot, combine peppercorns, tarragon, shallots, and wine. Simmer over medium heat until reduced by half. Strain reduced liquid into a blender or food processor. Discard solids. Add butter to hot liquid a few tablespoons at a time, blending until sauce is emulsified. Season with salt. Serve warm with blackened red drum or whatever seafood suits your fancy! Remaining sauce may be refrigerated for up to 3 days. Reheat before serving.

PEAR–VANILLA BEAN SANGRIA
Yields 1 pitcher

1½ cups water
1½ cups sugar
4 pears, peeled, cored, and halved
½ vanilla bean
2 cups dry white wine
½ cup pear vodka
½ cup brandy
1½ cups lemon-lime soda
1½ cups soda water
Pear slices for garnish
Fresh mint for garnish

In a medium saucepan, boil water with sugar until sugar dissolves. Add pears and ½ vanilla bean. Simmer for 20 minutes until pears are soft. Cool, remove vanilla bean, and purée mixture in a blender until smooth. (Vanilla bean pod may be rinsed and reserved for other use.) Add wine, vodka, and brandy. Fill a pitcher with ice, then add pear mixture until pitcher is half full. Add equal parts lemon-lime soda and soda water to fill pitcher. Garnish with pear slices and mint.

Todd Whitney
at J. Betski's

J. Betski's
    10 West Franklin St.
    Suite 120, Seaboard Station
    Raleigh, N.C. 27604
    919-833-7999
www.jbetskis.com
Directions
    From Durham or Chapel Hill, take I-40 East to Exit
    289, then follow Wade Avenue to Glenwood Avenue.
    Turn right, go to West Peace Street, turn left, go to
    Halifax Street, turn left, and go to West Franklin
    Street. J. Betski's is on the left at the end of the short
    street.
Cuisine
    This restaurant serves Central European cuisine with
    an emphasis on German and Polish dishes.

When Executive Chef Todd Whitney traveled the world as a child, he knew even then he wanted to be a cook. "At a young age, I decided I wanted to be in a restaurant cooking. I cooked for the family and got cookbooks very early. I made profiteroles—cream puffs—when I was ten," he says.

Because his father was an executive with Nortel, Todd traveled

Todd Whitney

a lot. At the age of eight, he moved with his family to Japan for three years. When he was ten and eleven, he went to Hong Kong, Thailand, Malaysia, Singapore, China, and Europe. "These travels opened my eyes to the experiences of different cultures and different foods. I became not so intimidated. Traveling was the defining experience in my life. It's what makes me tick. I like different cultures, different foods," Todd says.

But through it all, "Mom's food is still the best."

Todd was born in Raleigh and attended school there. He worked in restaurants for years but was "in denial." He tried college at Appalachian State University. During the summer of 1996, he worked at Grandfather Golf and Country Club near Linville. A chef there "became a mentor to me," says Todd. "He told me to think hard about becoming a chef but suggested culinary schools anyway."

Todd "hated going to class, hated writing papers. I couldn't imagine sitting at a desk for the rest of my life." So he went to Western Culinary Institute in Oregon "to get out of North Carolina for a while."

After culinary school, his training as a chef really began. He worked at Mille Fleurs in San Diego, California, with Chef Martin Woesle, "a German in a French restaurant who had trained at Michelin Three Star restaurants." The work was grueling. "The boss was a very exacting person, but he got me to where I am now. They had a farm down the road, and we got vegetables from there. We got in whole fish. Antelope. Live shrimp. It was the first time I had seen those things," says Todd.

From there, Todd returned to Raleigh to work at Bistro 607. He met John Korzekwinski, a man with a German and Polish heritage who had dreamed for years of opening a restaurant. While Todd cooked, Korzekwinski prepped during the day and waited tables at night. He talked with a passion about the foods he wanted to serve in his restaurant. Todd told him, "Oh, yeah. I've done that before." Korzekwinski and Todd became such good friends that their partnering in a new restaurant came about naturally.

When the time came to open the restaurant, named for one of Korzekwinski's grandparents, Todd, Korzekwinski, and the general manager put in sweat equity. "John and I had quit Bistro 607 and were waiting for this place to open. I personally painted beams, stained the bar and doors, and caulked the kitchen," says Todd. "The boxes came with all our equipment, and there were stickers on everything. We had to soak them and peel them off. Opening a restaurant is a unique experience."

Table settings at J. Betski's

Todd specializes in Central European cuisine—Czech, Austrian, and others. He "pores through history books and cookbooks. The food and history is all intermingled."

The staff makes everything in-house, including sausages, sourdough rye bread, the pretzels for the pretzel-encrusted pork—everything except some mustards and jams. Both Todd and Korzekwinski make the sausages, among them duck and cherry sausage, bratwurst, knackwurst, and smoked beef and pork kielbasa.

"We make spaetzle, served with ham, for example. It's old-school and rustic," says Todd. "But we have fancy plates. It's a well-grounded cuisine. Something you can sink your teeth into." He adds, "We use fresh local ingredients. The farmers come by as well as local meat producers—pigs, chicken, occasionally venison. I find braising of the cheaper cuts of meat fascinating."

J. Betski's is an intimate restaurant, but Chef Todd and Korzekwinski make the dining experience large.

Executive Chef Todd Whitney's Recipes

PRETZEL-CRUSTED PORK TENDERLOIN, COOKED SAUERKRAUT, AND BEER JUS

Serves 4

Pretzel Crust

½ cup melted butter
⅓ cup grated Parmesan Reggiano
10 pretzel rods, broken into small pieces (J. Betski's uses
    homemade pretzels, but store-bought ones will suffice)
¼ cup grainy Dijon mustard
1 tablespoon honey

In a food processor, pulse butter with cheese and pretzels to
form a chunky crust. Separately, combine mustard and honey
to form a "glue" for the crust. Reserve.

Pork Tenderloins

Salt and white pepper to taste
4 2-ounce pork tenderloin medallions

Preheat oven to 425 degrees. Add salt and white pepper to
all sides of medallions. Sear medallions for 3 minutes on both
flat ends in a sauté pan over medium heat. Smear mustard
"glue" on 1 side of medallions and pack pretzel crust on top
of "glue." Finish in oven for 3 to 5 minutes until crust is golden
brown and pork is cooked medium-well.

Cooked Sauerkraut

1 cup double-smoked bacon, diced medium
½ cup duck fat (available from a butcher) or lard
1 onion, julienned
1 tablespoon caraway seeds
4 cups sauerkraut (J. Betski's makes its own, but Hengstenberg
    is a good canned kraut; the varieties in bags with liquid in
    them are also good)
4 cloves
8 juniper berries
2 bay leaves

¾ cup white wine
¾ cup beef stock
4 tablespoons flour

Cook bacon in duck fat or lard in a large, deep saucepan over medium heat until golden brown. Add onions and cook until slightly brown. Add caraway seeds and stir. Add sauerkraut, straining and reserving juice. Sauté, continuing to stir. Add cloves, juniper berries, bay leaves, and wine. Bring to a boil, then add beef stock and a splash of sauerkraut juice. Bring to a boil again, then cover and cook over medium heat for about 30 to 45 minutes. Sauerkraut should be soft and tender, not crunchy, and should have absorbed some liquid. Add flour, stir, and cook 2 more minutes. Sauerkraut should have the consistency of a thick stew, slightly runny yet slightly dense. It should hold its shape when plated, yet ooze around the edges.

Beer Jus

2 cloves garlic, peeled and cut in half
3 shallots, julienned
1 tablespoon canola oil
2 12-ounce bottles dark German beer such as Spaten
 Optimator
4 cloves
10 black peppercorns
1 bay leaf
2 cups beef stock
Salt to taste
Juice of ½ lemon

Sweat garlic and shallots in canola oil. Add beer, cloves, peppercorns, and bay leaf and reduce by ¾. Add beef stock and reduce by half again. Sauce should barely coat the back of a spoon. Add salt and lemon juice. Strain and set aside. Discard solids.

To plate, place pretzel-encrusted medallions on top of cooked sauerkraut. Pour beer jus around the sides.

Cary

Michael Chuong

Michael Chuong
at Ân

Ân
2800 Renaissance Park Pl.
Cary, N.C. 27513
919-677-9229
info@ancuisines.com
www.ancuicines.com
Directions
From Raleigh, take I-40 West to Exit 287 toward Cary.
Turn onto North Harrison Avenue, go to Weston
Parkway, and turn right. Go to the first stoplight, at
Renaissance Park Place, and turn left. Ân is on the
corner on the left. Parking is on the premises. From
Durham or Chapel Hill, take I-40 East to Exit 287
toward Cary. Turn onto North Harrison Avenue, go
to Weston Parkway, and turn right. Go to the first
stoplight, at Renaissance Park Place, and turn left. Ân
is on the corner on the left.
Cuisine
This chef-owned restaurant serves New World
cuisine—a fusion of Vietnamese, French, and other
influences. It offers sushi and a raw bar.

Executive Chef Michael Chuong presides over his own restaurant,
Ân, after years of working for others. Ân features cuisines that Michael
studied throughout his extensive training. The building that houses
the restaurant, located at a busy Cary intersection, offers the peace and

beauty inherent in each of Michael's styles of food—Vietnamese, French, sushi, and raw bar selections. But it hides the truth of a journey based on courage, creativity, inventiveness, and a love of the cooking profession.

At the age of fifteen in 1978, the year before Michael was to become eligible for the draft in Vietnam, his parents paid for his and his sister's passage on an American merchant marine ship on its way to Singapore. "Millions of people died in the ocean, but I was very fortunate. Singapore was the best refugee camp," Michael says.

The brother and sister ended up in New Orleans under the sponsorship of the American Catholic Church. They were placed in an orphanage and went to public high schools. Michael, who had his "heart set on becoming an architect," attended Louisiana State University for three years before he encountered the love of his life, cooking.

He had no funds, and summer jobs were a must. In 1985, a friend found him work in the kitchen of the New Orleans InterContinental Hotel, one of a chain of four- and five-star international hotels. He worked under a traditional French chef, Andre Billion Tarrard. "When I started, I didn't know what a club sandwich looked like, but I did everything they asked me to do. I worked in the pantry, squeezing two cases of orange juice every night and peeling boxes of garlic," Michael says.

He was ready to go back to the university after three months. Then "the chef said, 'Michael, you do very well in the kitchen. I can train you. I can send you to in-house training.' And I had no parents, no ties, so I said, 'Sure, for one semester.' A year after I started, I was *sous chef*, and two years later I was promoted at age twenty-five to *chef de cuisine* at the InterContinental Hotel's five-star restaurant, Les Continents," Michael says.

Many famous French chefs such as Paul Bocuse came through the hotel, but the most influential cook in Chef Michael's life was his mother. Back in Vietnam, she studied cooking before she married. "I still learn a lot from her. She inspired me about cooking, about making things look nice." His parents now live in New York's large Asian community. Michael and his sister saved up enough money to sponsor them to come to the United States in the 1980s.

After Michael spent two years as *chef de cuisine* at Les Continents, he worked with a friend who opened a new restaurant, Delargo, which received a four-star review from the *New Orleans Times-Picayune* newspaper. When his friend sold the business, Michael joined the four-star Fairmont Hotel,

Dining area at Ân

working in its Sazerac dining room. In 1995, he accepted the position of executive chef and operations manager at City Energy Club of America. But by then, New Orleans had become too crowded for his family, which included two young daughters.

When Prestonwood Country Club made him "an offer I couldn't refuse," he moved his family to Cary, which offers "much better schools." The country club—owned by Jim Goodnight, CEO of the SAS software company, and his wife, Ann—was a big operation. "So many things going on at the same time. They had two thousand members, which means eight-thousand-plus people," Michael says. It was difficult for him to focus on his New World cuisine—a fusion of French and Asian influences—but he experimented and caught Ann Goodnight's attention.

"Mrs. Goodnight did a lot for my education. She said, 'Michael, I want you to pick out a place anywhere in the world to study, and I'll pay for it.' She always encouraged me to go," Michael says. As a consequence, he studied under prestigious chefs and native cooks in Thailand and Vietnam and at the Sushi Academy in California, all the while perfecting his New World cuisine.

"One day in 2003, Mrs. Goodnight said, 'I want to open a restaurant for you,' " he says. And she did. "The whole concept, the theme, came from me," says Michael. They took trips all over the United States looking for the right designer before choosing Paul Draper from Dallas, who conferred with Michael about his concept, his vision, and his background. The result is Ân, a word that means "to eat" in Vietnamese.

"I'm not Thai, not Vietnamese, not Asian. This is Chef Michael. Unique. Classical European, Japanese, Chinese, Southeast Asian—all fusion," Michael says. "Asian fusion is four hundred to five hundred years old. The French occupied Vietnam for over one hundred years. Prior to that, there were a lot of French and European influences in Vietnam."

So, thanks to his study of classical French cuisine in the first years he cooked, and thanks to his Vietnamese heritage, Michael practices "a more authentic, more honest fusion than other chefs can do," he says.

"Each dish is unique," he says. "I use the best-quality ingredients, so that each dish has its own flavor profile. You have to understand the product and where it comes from."

The wine cellars at Ân reflect the fusion theme. They contain over 2,200 bottles, 360 varietals, and the largest premium sake collection in the Triangle. The wines are from Spain, Italy, France, California, Australia, and South Africa, among other places.

Ân is designed to complement Michael's profile as a chef—creative and inventive. Throughout the space are sophisticated and beautiful art pieces and antiques to accompany the architecture, which has echoes of French colonial and Eastern themes. It is a space where the classical foundation of New World dishes is at home.

"Creating these dishes is a very fun thing to do. I'm like a chemist, putting things together so it becomes something new, something wonderful. I guess few people have that opportunity," Chef Michael says.

Executive Chef Michael Chuong's Recipes

WALNUT PRAWNS

Serves 4

Sauce
1 cup mayonnaise
¼ cup honey
2 tablespoons whole-grain mustard
Sriracha (Asian hot sauce)

Combine ingredients in a large bowl. Use *sriracha* sparingly; add to taste.

Shrimp
Vegetable oil for frying
2 pounds extra jumbo shrimp (16/20 count), peeled and
    deveined
½ cup egg whites (from approximately 4 large eggs), beaten
1½ cups cornstarch
1 cup whole walnuts for garnish
Cooked brown or white rice

In a deep skillet, place enough oil to cover shrimp. Heat oil to 350 degrees. Coat shrimp in egg whites. Be sure to drain excess whites. Place cornstarch in a shallow bowl. Move shrimp to cornstarch and coat thoroughly. Using tongs, gently place shrimp in batches in oil so skillet is not crowded. Cook for 2 to

3 minutes until cooked through, turning once. Place shrimp on a plate covered with paper towels to remove excess oil. Toss shrimp in sauce until thoroughly covered. Toast walnuts in a 350-degree oven for 10 to 15 minutes until lightly browned.

To serve, place 8 shrimp on each of 4 plates, garnish with toasted walnuts, and serve with a side of rice.

VIET ROLLS
Serves 4

Peanut Dipping Sauce
2 teaspoons chopped garlic
1 teaspoon fresh lemon grass, white parts only
1 tablespoon vegetable oil
2 tablespoons chunky peanut butter
2 tablespoons hoisin sauce (Asian sweet plum sauce)
½ cup water
1 teaspoon sambal (Asian garlic-chili hot sauce)
1 teaspoon vinegar
2 teaspoons coconut milk from fresh coconut or canned coconut milk

Sauté garlic and lemon grass in oil until brown. Mix in peanut butter, hoisin sauce, and water. Bring to a boil and stir in sambal, vinegar, and coconut milk.

Rolls
2 ounces pork loin
Salt and pepper to taste
4 shrimp
4 tapioca papers (Vietnamese spring roll papers)
¼ cup organic greens such as raw spinach leaves, stems removed
4 or more mint leaves
¼ cup cooked rice noodles, salted to taste
½ cup fresh bean sprouts
¼ cup cucumber, julienned

Preheat oven to 350 degrees. Season pork with salt and pepper. Roast in oven in a greased pan for about 15 minutes until well done. Allow pork to cool, then slice into pieces 2 inches in length and ⅓ to ½ inch wide. Boil shrimp about 3 minutes until pink and cooked. Place in an ice bath. Peel, devein, and slice in half lengthwise. Wet tapioca papers in simmering water about 1 minute until pliable. Remove with a flat sieve or a slotted spoon. Working quickly, lay papers on flat, moistened surfaces such as dinner plates. Using 1 paper at a time, arrange greens on bottom third of paper. Put 3 pieces of pork, 2 pieces of shrimp, 1 or more mint leaves, a small clump of rice noodles, bean sprouts, and cucumbers on top. Fold bottom portion of paper over filling. Fold in left and right sides, then roll paper until completely wrapped. Be sure to roll tightly until edges seal shut. Place finished rolls on a plate and cover with a damp towel to keep moist until serving time.

·····················

To serve, place peanut dipping sauce in a small, shallow dish. Dip rolls in sauce or spoon sauce over rolls.

Scott Crawford

Scott Crawford
at Herons (Umstead Hotel and Spa)

Herons at the Umstead Hotel and Spa
5 SAS Campus Dr.
100 Woodland Pond
Cary, N.C. 27513
919-447-4000
www.heronsrestaurant.com

Directions

From Raleigh, take I-40 West to Exit 287 toward Cary
and turn onto North Harrison Avenue. After passing over
I-40, take the first left onto SAS Campus Drive. The hotel
is on the left. From Durham or Chapel Hill, take I-40
East to Exit 287 toward Cary. Turn onto North Harrison
Avenue and take first left onto SAS Campus Drive. The
hotel is on the left.

Cuisine

This AAA Four Diamond, Mobil Four Star restaurant
serves modern American cuisine with Southern
influences using fresh local ingredients.

Executive Chef Scott Crawford grew up in farm country north of
Pittsburgh, Pennsylvania. He worked on a farm as a boy during the
summers.

His most significant taste memory came when he was given a slice
of an heirloom tomato grown by his grandfather. At the age of six, Scott

found it "the ugliest thing I ever saw." But it was also "the most amazing thing I've ever tasted." The balance of sweet and acidic enthralled him. Then they "sliced the tomato, put it on warm, just-baked bread, put some mayonnaise on it, added a little salt." It is a taste memory that guides him today.

By the age of seventeen, the creative, independent young man was ready to leave Pennsylvania and head south to Florida, where his mother lived. He attended junior college in Tallahassee and worked in a restaurant to earn money. He began to assess his goals for a career—"teaching, intensity, managing, and balance." A chef he shared this list with said, "You can do all those things cooking." That was when he chose to attend the American Culinary Academy in Tampa, a small college that no longer exists. "I got a lot out of it," Scott says. He did his externship with the prominent chef Scott Howard at Mise en Place in Tampa. Howard then hired Scott as *sous chef* and told him to do a *stage* at Norman's in Miami with Chef Norman Van Aken.

From there, Scott went to San Francisco to work with Chef Reed Heron at the upscale French bistro Black Cat. But in a move that pointed him toward his role as hotel executive chef, he joined the Ritz Carlton, opening restaurants for the company in new hotels. The Ritz Carlton, says Scott, "was one of the best hotel companies in the world at that time. It was my doctorate, if you will."

He went to the Woodlands Resort & Inn and "oversaw the entire operation." There, he understood that overseeing a hotel's dining operations was his passion. However, he accepted an offer to take the Grill Room at Amelia Island Resort from the development stage to a AAA Five Diamond restaurant. He did so in eighteen months.

His move to Herons at the Umstead Hotel and Spa seemed a natural development for Scott. "I wanted to be in hotel operations, but I love cooking, love touching food every day. Here, I oversee banquets, the spa cuisine, and stewarding," he says.

His cuisine is modern American. "A lot of my generation are American-trained chefs. I learned how to cook with experiences throughout the country." Furthermore, he says, "modern American cuisine celebrates diversity. It's a melting pot. There's a borrowing of techniques from the French to the Spanish. I think that what each modern American chef does with that is intriguing."

Scott's cuisine is also Southern. "That's what grounds me. I'm grounded

Dining area at Heron's

by what my guests can relate to—hams, fish, all the great vegetables grown in the South," he says.

An example of his Southern-inflected cuisine is his salad of Bibb lettuce, Easter egg radishes, and buttermilk vinaigrette. He also mixes Old Country cuisine with Southern in his ham ravioli dish with fava beans and morels.

Before he agreed to come to North Carolina, he had heard about Durham's Magnolia Grill and the emerging food scene. "I knew North Carolina was beautiful and that there's a change of seasons. I missed that living in Georgia and Florida," he says. "My wife and I already feel at home here. It was the warmest welcome we've ever experienced."

Scott, like many chefs in this book, is a perfectionist. "I start with the basics: how to fold towels, how to keep the station organized, how you keep your floor clean. I teach my team to organize so they're operating at maximum efficiency. All this comes through in the cuisine," he says. "This is what I teach my team. The flow, flavors, and balance will come together for them then."

As at the beginning of his search for a career, balance is vital to Scott's cuisine. "I balance flavors, textures, colors, fats, acidity, and saltiness. When you learn to balance, people say, like I did with my grandfather's tomatoes, 'Wow.' I always use the best local products. Harvest in the morning, have it on the plate in the evening." A farmer has agreed to set aside two acres for the hotel, which already has an herb garden for the dining room.

Working in an open kitchen in an elegant, sophisticated dining room amid hotel owner Ann Goodnight's art collection is like a dream come true. All in all, Chef Scott thinks that North Carolina is a great place to be with his wife and young son.

Executive Chef Scott Crawford's Recipes

CHEDDAR GRITS SOUFFLÉ WITH TOMATOES AND SHRIMP AND SMOKED PEPPER-BACON JUS
Note: Make the grits soufflé last, so it will be warm at serving.

Serves 6

Smoked Pepper-Bacon Jus
Makes 1 cup
1 tablespoon butter
2 slices smoked bacon
½ cup chopped onion
½ cup red bell pepper, seeded and chopped
1 tablespoon tomato paste
8 black peppercorns
1 bay leaf
1 sprig thyme
1 clove garlic, chopped
1 quart chicken stock

Salt to taste
1 tablespoon cornstarch
1 tablespoon water

In a medium saucepan, brown butter over medium heat, then add bacon and brown slightly. Add onions and red bell peppers and cook until they begin to slightly caramelize. Add tomato paste and coat vegetables evenly, stirring for 1 minute. Add peppercorns, bay leaf, thyme, garlic, and chicken stock and simmer gently. Reduce liquid by half. Adjust salt. Mix cornstarch and water together, then stir into sauce, stirring often. Cook for about 5 minutes until starch cooks out and mixture ceases to be cloudy, then strain through a fine sieve. Reserve sauce and keep hot.

Tomatoes and Shrimp

24 grape tomatoes
12 shrimp (10-20 count), peeled and deveined
1 shallot, diced
¼ cup chicken stock
2 tablespoons cold butter
Salt and pepper to taste

To peel tomatoes, submerge them in ice water for 2 minutes, remove them, and drop them in boiling water for 10 seconds. Remove from water and place back into ice water. The skins should just peel off.

Skewer shrimp on small bamboo skewers. Poach in salted simmering water for about 1 minute until just barely cooked. Chill in ice water and remove from skewers. Cut shrimp into disks ¼ inch thick and reserve.

In a sauté pan, bring chicken stock to a gentle simmer and add shrimp and tomatoes. Add butter, swirling it until it emulsifies into the stock. Season with salt and pepper.

Cheddar Grits

Makes 2 cups
½ cup stone-ground grits
1½ cups ham or chicken stock
1 teaspoon salt
1 cup heavy cream

4 tablespoons butter
1 cup shredded sharp cheddar cheese

In a medium saucepan over low heat, add grits, stock, salt, cream, and butter. Bring to a simmer and cook for approximately 1 hour, stirring often, until tender. Fold in cheese and allow to cool to room temperature.

Grits Soufflé

4 egg yolks
1 teaspoon cornstarch
2 egg whites

Preheat oven to 375 degrees. Butter six 4-ounce ramekins. In a large stainless-steel mixing bowl, combine 1 cup of cooled cheddar grits, yolks, and cornstarch. Reserve.

When you are ready to cook soufflés, whisk egg whites to medium peaks, then fold into grits mixture in 3 parts. Do not overmix, as it will deflate egg whites. Place mixture into ramekins so they are ¾ full. Bake for 10 to 12 minutes until tips are a rich golden brown and slightly firm to the touch. Remove from oven and with an oven mitt or towel turn soufflés out onto center of each of 6 plates.

To serve, arrange shrimp around soufflés, alternating 2 slices of shrimp to 1 tomato. To finish, pour jus over soufflés and enjoy!

Hillsborough

Aaron Vandemark

Aaron Vandemark
at Panciuto

Panciuto
110 South Churton St.
Hillsborough, N.C. 27278
919-732-7261
www.panciuto.com
Directions
From Raleigh, take I-40 West to Exit 261. Turn left
(north) to eventually merge onto South Churton Street
in Hillsborough. Go several blocks to Panciuto, on the
left across from the courthouse. From Chapel Hill, take
N.C. 86 North to Meadowland Court in Hillsborough.
Turn left, go to South Churton Street, turn right, and
continue to Panciuto, on the left. From Durham, take
I-85 West to Exit 164. Turn right onto South Churton
Street in Hillsborough and go several blocks to
Panciuto, on the left.
Cuisine
This chef-owned restaurant serves Italian cuisine with a
Southern inflection, featuring local produce and meats.

After spending the first years of his life in New York, Chef Aaron
Vandemark came with his parents to the Durham–Chapel Hill area when
he was ten. Now, as an adult, he thinks of himself as a North Carolinian,
which is pertinent to the way he cooks. He seeks out local farmers and
meat producers and presents his Italian cuisine with care and extreme
thoughtfulness. For example, he uses only fresh farmers' market tomatoes
in his tomato sauce.

Dining room of Panciuto

Though customers may not always recognize it, Aaron is conscious of the long journey the food took to get from the ground to the table. And that awareness is a large part of Panciuto's purpose. The preparation and presentation of the food show that consciousness. Aaron features local, fresh ingredients on his menu. Everything is made in-house. The menu changes seasonally with offerings such as Sweet Potato *Francobolli* with Fried Goat Cheese, Wilted Collard Strings, Pecans, and Truffle Aioli.

Aaron's training includes a degree in economics from Emory University that he earned while making the decision to become a chef. "I worked in an office after my junior year in college, but at night I worked in a restaurant. I went home, lost the suit, put on scrubs. The contrast between jobs was clear to me. I figured out I wasn't going to be in an office," he says.

He decided that if he was going to be in the restaurant business, "I needed to do it right. I got a job at Il Palio with Chef Gennaro Villella. The work with him was all-consuming." After nine months with Chef Villella, he went to culinary school at Johnson & Wales in Norfolk, Virginia. However, "the cook I am today is a product of where I worked, what I learned from the chefs, reading, messing up, and getting things right," he says.

Aaron continued his training at Fearrington House Restaurant for a summer. The chefs there, including Chef Graham Fox, "added new influences. It was the first place where I went to the garden and cut flowers for the plate." For a while, he worked in catering at a university, which was a different type of experience. "I decided I didn't want that," he says.

One of his most formative experiences was the eleven months he spent at Magnolia Grill doing daytime prep. It was an opportunity to learn while he worked on his project of opening Panciuto. But he wants to make it clear that he "learned from working with Magnolia Grill chef Ben Barker. I was not under him. I learned how to reinforce good habits, how to use fresh produce, and proper cooking techniques. That experience solidified the direction I was going in."

Opening Panciuto in a small town has had its challenges and rewards. The creative aspect of cooking appeals to Aaron, who is an artist. He says, "There are three rewards. The immediate satisfaction of cooking something that's greater than the sum of its parts. You get to feed people, and they enjoy your food. And there's the monetary reward for doing something you like."

But the aspect that brings Aaron the most satisfaction is the closeness he has with area farmers. "They bring me their food, their raw ingredients, and I get to do whatever I want with it. It's a process that begins in the ground and with animals that are raised humanely and with love," he says.

Aaron's cuisine is Italian, based on his early experience at Il Palio. "People enjoy Italian food." The cuisine, he says, "is straightforward. Presentation is not that important to me because we take great produce and meats and combine them in an interesting way."

He says, "Local food is one of the pillars of what this restaurant stands on—local farmers and local products. I believe that if we provide a great product, people will come out and eat it."

Everything is made in-house—the bacon, cured products, breads, desserts. And Panciuto has a distinct family quality, since Chef Aaron's wife, parents, and sister all give a hand to help out.

Panciuto—meaning "pot belly"—is named in memory of a cherished pet. Its forty-one seats are often filled on the weekends with customers coming from Chapel Hill, Durham, Raleigh, and Pittsboro, as well as from Hillsborough.

Chef Aaron Vandemark's Recipes

PARMESAN ANCHOVY DRESSING
Yields 2 cups

1 anchovy from can or jar, packed in oil
2 egg yolks (pasteurized yolks may be substituted)
3 tablespoons freshly squeezed lemon juice
1 teaspoon Dijon mustard
1 teaspoon garlic, roughly chopped
½ teaspoon Worcestershire sauce
½ cup extra-virgin olive oil
½ cup canola oil
⅞ cup grated Parmesan cheese
1 tablespoon water
Salt and pepper to taste

Put anchovy, yolks, lemon juice, Dijon, garlic, and Worcestershire in a food processor and blend to combine well. Combine olive oil and canola oil in a measuring cup, reserving ¼ cup of oil mixture in a separate cup. Very slowly pour ¾ cup of oil into a food processor while it is running. If you add oil too quickly, you will break the emulsion and mixture will look oily. If it stays smooth and creamy, you have properly emulsified the mixture. Add Parmesan and water. Add reserved ¼ cup of oil, again pouring slowly. Season with salt and pepper and serve on salad of your choice. Dressing may be refrigerated for up to 3 days.

BONET

Bonet is a chocolate flan pudding from northern Italy.

Serves 6

Caramel

1 cup sugar
¼ cup water
6 amaretto cookies

Place sugar and water in a medium saucepan over medium to medium-high heat, stirring occasionally until sugar melts and mixture reaches a rich caramel color. This process may take 10 minutes, depending on heat. Remember that caramel at this point is like molten lava; do not touch or splash. Use caramel immediately. Carefully pour a little into six 8-ounce individual ramekins and swirl quickly to coat bottoms. Mixture will set quickly, so working with a partner can help. Once caramel has set, crumble enough amaretto cookies over caramel to cover bottoms of ramekins.

These steps can be done ahead of time. Caramel will keep until you are ready to proceed with custard (flan) portion of recipe.

Flan

1½ cups cream
½ cup milk
½ cinnamon stick, crushed
½ teaspoon cocoa powder

½ vanilla bean, scraped (bean and pod may be reserved for
   other use)
1 cup sugar, divided
3 egg yolks
1 egg
¼ teaspoon salt
½ tablespoon rum

Preheat oven to 325 degrees. In a saucepan, mix cream, milk, cinnamon, cocoa, vanilla bean, and ½ cup of the sugar. Heat over medium heat to just boiling. Shut off heat and steep for 30 minutes.

Whisk yolks, egg, remaining ½ cup sugar, and salt in a bowl. Add rum. Add steeped cream mixture slowly in a very thin stream to egg mixture, whisking all the while. Whisk lightly to smooth. Strain through a fine strainer. Ladle custard into ramekins over crushed cookies, which will float to the top. Place ramekins in a baking pan about 2 inches deep. Place on oven rack and pour boiling water into baking pan to reach halfway up ramekins. Cover with foil and bake for 20 to 25 minutes.

Remove from oven, being careful not to slosh water into ramekins. Chill thoroughly.

To serve, carefully run the tip of a knife around edges of ramekins and invert onto a serving platter. With a little effort, they will pop out and ooze caramel.

Pittsboro

Colin Bedford

Colin Bedford
at Fearrington House Restaurant
(Fearrington House Country Inn)

Fearrington House Restaurant at
Fearrington House Country Inn
2000 Fearrington Village
Pittsboro, N.C. 27312
919-542-2121
fhouse@fearrington.com
www.fearrington.com
Directions
From Raleigh, take I-40 West to Exit 273, then follow
U.S. 15/501 South to Fearrington Village, on the left.
Take the first right after entering the village. From
Durham or Chapel Hill, take U.S. 15/501 Business
South past Chapel Hill. At N.C. 54, exit right and turn
left to stay on U.S. 15/501. Continue to Fearrington
Village, on the left. Take the first right after entering the
village.
Cuisine
This AAA Five Diamond restaurant, a member of
Relais & Châteaux and a Certified Green Restaurant,
serves new North American cuisine with regional and
seasonal ingredients.

Executive Chef Colin Bedford began cooking when he was fourteen.
Living in a home where his "mum" cooked every single meal, he would
often wake up to scones, fairy cakes, and Victorian sponge cakes. His

father had a plot of land, an allotment, on which he grew onions, potatoes, and beans. Good food was part of Colin's growing up.

So it was natural that he would study hotel management and earn a degree in hospitality from his local college, Yeovil College in Somerset in the southwest of England. At the age of eighteen, degree in hand, he went to the Castle Hotel, one of Europe's leading family-run hotels and one of England's finest dining establishments. He began working there in 1996. It was then that the young man met Chef Graham Fox.

In 2000, Colin left the Castle Hotel at the same time Chef Fox left to join Fearrington House Restaurant. But Colin went to Canada to join the staff at the Prince of Wales Hotel, a CAA/AAA Four Diamond hotel and restaurant. He served as junior *sous chef* and stayed for five years, leaving in 2005 to visit Executive Chef Fox in Fearrington Village. Their paths had crossed again.

"I was interested in coming down here, and when I came I discovered that North Carolina is different. It's slower-paced, and it's a great location—mountains, beaches, close to the airport," Colin says.

Chef Fox recruited him to become executive *sous chef* at Fearrington House Restaurant. And when Fox left the AAA Five Diamond restaurant in 2008, Colin naturally became his replacement.

It is clear why Colin was named executive chef. "My philosophy of food preparation is that simplicity is the key to maximum flavors. Less is more. That's a very hard thing for a chef to do—to hold back, to not keep adding more flavors," he says. "I keep the food simple, but with a twist. For example, I made a recipe that's Peanut Butter Parfait with Strawberry Jam Ice Cream. Simple, recognizable, but with a twist." He adds, "I like comfort food, and we present it so it's a beautiful construction. People connect to familiar items. They can relate to what's familiar on the menu."

Colin says, "People eat with their eyes. If it looks good, you've won them over from the get-go." Colin's presentations give the food an irresistible impact. That, together with the fact that he likes substantial food, "gives the guests value for their money," he says.

Colin's cuisine is new North American with regional and seasonal ingredients, though his background is European, French in particular. He preserves spring and summer fruits such as cherries and quince to serve with winter fare.

"Here, I had my first insight into farm-to-table cooking. We have a vegetable garden out back. We harvest them when the vegetables are tiny

Interior of Fearrington House Restaurant

because of the impact of presentation," Colin says.

R. B. Fitch, who developed Fearrington Village, plays a role in the restaurant. Colin says that he and "Mr. Fitch are on the same page." Fitch told Colin there are two Bs in the restaurant: bread and breakfast. Bread is the first thing guests put in their mouths, and breakfast is the first meal of the day. Both stick in their memories.

Fitch also told Colin not to touch Thanksgiving and Christmas. He said that people have expectations about those meals, and that the restaurant should strive to meet them.

Everything is made in-house, including the bread. Most products come from local farmers.

Colin has learned an important lesson living in North Carolina. "People are genuine," he says. And he has learned to read the needs of his chefs. "Different people have different needs." He adds, "I'm only as good as my staff in the kitchen. They are a great bunch of guys. It's a respect thing. They respect me, and I respect them."

Colin creates the recipes that the restaurant serves. He and his executive *sous chef* check every plate that goes out to guests. If it is not perfect, they send it back.

Fearrington House Restaurant and Executive Chef Colin Bedford earn every diamond they get from AAA.

·····:::::::::::::·····

Note

R. B. Fitch, a native of Chapel Hill, began developing Fearrington Village in the early 1970s after he and his late wife, Jenny, purchased the 640-acre dairy farm from Jesse Fearrington. The farm had been in the Fearrington family since 1786. Ironically, in the late 1970s, R. B. and Jenny invited a young couple eager to open a French restaurant to be the first restaurateurs. They were Chef Bill Neal and his wife, Moreton. The Neals brought not only memorable food but also the tradition that Fearrington Village would nurture outstanding restaurants and excellent chefs. The Fitches continued to bring exceptional chefs to the restaurant, including legendary Southern chef Edna Lewis and Walter Royal, the current executive chef at Angus Barn. They also invited Ben Barker and Karen Barker, who stayed for five years until 1986, then left to open their own restaurant, Magnolia Grill.

Executive Chef Colin Bedford's Recipes

BACON-WRAPPED CHICKEN BREAST, SAVOY CABBAGE, AND SAGE RISOTTO

Serves 6

2 cups water
2 tablespoons loose-leaf jasmine tea
1 cup raisins
2 quarts chicken stock
2 shallots, chopped
1 clove garlic, chopped
1 tablespoon butter
Pinch of salt
3 cups Arborio rice
2 cups white wine
6 strips bacon per chicken breast (about 1 pound)
3 skinless, boneless chicken breasts, cut horizontally through
    the middle but not all the way, then opened like a book
¾ cup seasoned ground bulk sausage
1 small head Savoy cabbage, thinly sliced
1 cup cream
2 tablespoons chopped fresh sage
½ cup chopped green onions
½ cup toasted pecans, roughly chopped
1 cup grated Parmesan cheese
⅔ cup mascarpone cheese

Bring 2 cups water to a boil and infuse with loose tea. Allow to stand for 30 minutes, then reheat tea, strain over raisins, and place to the side until raisins are plump. (You can do this in advance and reserve in refrigerator.)

Place chicken stock in a saucepan over medium heat. Sweat shallots and garlic in butter on low to medium heat in another saucepan. Add salt. Once shallots and garlic are soft and without color, add rice. Cook rice on a consistent medium heat until tips start to go translucent. Add wine and reduce by half.

Add half of warmed stock a ladle at a time. Add more only when rice has totally absorbed stock. It is very important to keep a consistent heat. This will take about 15 to 20 minutes. When rice is almost cooked, add a ladle of cold water, scoop rice onto a tray, and score lines into rice, which will allow risotto to cool quickly.

Lay 6 bacon slices side by side, overlapping slightly, on buttered foil to form a square on which each chicken breast will lie. Place butterflied chicken on top of bacon. Position sausage in a line on front portion of chicken. Roll chicken and bacon around sausage to form a cylinder. When finished, sausage will be in center of chicken and bacon will be on the outside. Wrap chicken with foil and tightly twist ends of foil in opposite directions. Simmer in a large pan of water for 30 to 35 minutes until firm to the touch.

Bring a pot of salted water to a boil. Blanch cabbage in water for 30 seconds and refresh in ice water.

To finish, take chicken out of foil and crisp bacon on chicken in an oiled, preheated pan. Reheat rice by using some of the warmed stock (used for making risotto) and cream. The warmer the risotto gets, the thicker the rice will become.

Be careful not to add too much liquid, as you do not want a watery consistency. Add raisins, cabbage, sage, green onions, pecans, Parmesan, and mascarpone to risotto. Once you add mascarpone, do not reboil risotto. Slice chicken crosswise. Spoon risotto into pasta bowls or on plates and place sliced chicken on top.

HAZELNUT PRALINE AND ORANGE *SEMIFREDDO* AND SHORTBREAD

Semifreddo, Italian for "half cold," refers to any of various chilled or partially frozen desserts including cake, ice cream, fruit, custard, and whipped cream.

Serves 10

Semifreddo

1¼ cups sugar, divided
1 cup water
1 cup peeled hazelnuts or other nuts such as almonds
1 vanilla bean
4 large eggs, separated (use commercial egg yolks if desired, 1 ounce for 1 yolk)

Pinch of salt
2 cups heavy cream
Zest of 1 orange

Grease a baking tray or cookie sheet with a rim for when caramel is ready. Place 1 cup of the sugar in a saucepan.

Add water and heat over medium heat to melt sugar. When sugar is dissolved, water will be clear. Wipe sides of pan down, removing any sugar granules. Place on medium-high heat and boil at about 235 degrees, measuring with a candy thermometer, until sugar water reaches the soft-ball stage. When sugar reaches caramel stage, add nuts, pour mixture onto greased tray, and allow to cool. Edges will be uneven. Once hazelnut praline is at room temperature, break into pieces, place in a food processor, and pulse for about 2 minutes into a coarse powder. Reserve in an airtight container.

Split vanilla bean in half and scrape out seeds into a bowl. (Pod may be reserved for other use.) Add remaining ¼ cup sugar to bowl and mix with vanilla seeds until blended.

Whip egg whites in a bowl just until they are broken up. Add salt and continue beating until firm peaks form. Place bowl in refrigerator.

In a large bowl, add vanilla bean–sugar mixture to egg yolks and beat with an electric mixer or whisk until pale. Place in refrigerator.

In another bowl, beat heavy cream to soft peaks using an electric mixer or a whisk. Do not overwhip. Place in refrigerator.

Remove whites, yolks, and heavy cream from refrigerator. Add praline powder, orange zest, and whites into yolk mixture, folding in thoroughly. Once ingredients are ⅔ incorporated, gently fold in whipped cream. Immediately scoop into a container, cover with plastic wrap, and freeze until ready to serve.

Shortbread

1¾ sticks butter
6 tablespoons sugar
1 cup all-purpose flour
6 tablespoons cornstarch
Pinch of salt

Preheat oven to 350 degrees. Cream together butter and sugar until pale. Add flour, cornstarch, and salt and mix until a ball forms. Chill mixture, then roll out to ⅛-inch thickness between 2 pieces of parchment paper. Cut into desired shapes and sizes, place on a cookie sheet, and bake until golden brown.

Serve shortbread on individual dessert plates alongside bowls of *semifreddo*.

Chefs' Chefs

Karen and Ben Barker

Ben Barker and Karen Barker
at Magnolia Grill

Magnolia Grill
1002 Ninth St.
Durham, N.C. 27705
919-286-3609
www.magnoliagrill.net
Directions
From Raleigh, take I-40 West to Exit 279B (N.C. 147
North/Durham Freeway). Follow Durham Freeway to
Exit 14 (Swift Avenue/Duke East Campus). Turn right
at the light and continue across Main Street onto Broad
Street. At the third stoplight, turn left onto Markham
Avenue. Go to the next light, at Ninth Street, turn right,
and continue to Magnolia Grill, on the right. From
Chapel Hill, take U.S. 15/501 Business (Durham–
Chapel Hill Boulevard) to Exit 105B, then follow U.S.
15/501 Bypass North to Exit 108B (Durham Freeway
South/N.C. 147). Go to Exit 14 (Swift Avenue/Duke
East) and turn left at the light. Continue past Main Street
onto Broad Street. At the third stoplight, turn left onto
Markham Avenue. Go to the next light, at Ninth Street,
turn right, and continue to Magnolia Grill, on the right.
Cuisine
This chef-owned restaurant serves New Southern cuisine
with fresh local ingredients.

Ben Barker, born in North Carolina, returned to the state in 1981
after he and his wife, New Yorker Karen Barker, graduated from the
Culinary Institute of America. Ben went to Chapel Hill and La Résidence,

a restaurant founded by Chef Bill Neal and Moreton Neal. At that time, Moreton Neal owned and managed the restaurant. Bill Smith, the future Crook's Corner chef, worked there.

R. B. Fitch recognized Ben's talent and invited him to become the executive chef at Fearrington House Restaurant. He also invited Karen to become the pastry chef. While at Fearrington, Ben developed his "Cuisine of the New South" and the first all-American wine list in North Carolina. He was instrumental in gaining the Relais & Châteaux luxury hotel designation for Fearrington.

The Barkers stayed at Fearrington until they decided to open their own restaurant in 1986 in a former grocery story on Ninth Street in Durham. The intention was to open a neighborhood restaurant and gathering place. Magnolia Grill remains in that same space today.

Ben and Karen have influenced numerous cooks and chefs, many of whom you can read about in this book. And their influence extends to chefs and pastry chefs nationwide.

The numerous honors and awards they and the restaurant have garnered include *Gourmet*'s ongoing selection of Magnolia Grill as among the top fifty restaurants in the nation; it was named number eleven in the United States in 2006. The James Beard Award has gone to Ben for Best Chef in the Southeast and to Karen for Outstanding Pastry Chef. *Bon Appétit* also named Karen as Best Pastry Chef. Magnolia Grill was a semifinalist in the 2009 James Beard Award for Outstanding Restaurant.

The Barkers are active in charity fundraisers for Meals on Wheels, Make-a-Wish Foundation, and Magic Moments, among other organizations. They are also cookbook authors. *Not Afraid of Flavor: Recipes from Magnolia Grill*, by Ben Barker and Karen Barker, was published by the University of North Carolina Press in 2000. *Sweet Stuff: Karen Barker's American Desserts* was published by UNC Press in 2004.

Andrea Reusing
at Lantern

Lantern
423 West Franklin St.
Chapel Hill, N.C. 27516
919-969-8846
info@lanternrestaurant.com
www.lanternrestaurant.com
Directions
From Raleigh, take I-40 West to Exit 270 for U.S.
15/501 Business (Durham–Chapel Hill Boulevard).
Turn left at the light, continue on U.S. 15/501 to
Chapel Hill, and take the Franklin Street exit, to the
right. Continue on Franklin Street past Columbia
Street to West Franklin Street. Lantern is on the left.
Valet parking is available across the street. From
Durham, take U.S. 15/501 Business to Chapel Hill and
the Franklin Street exit. Follow the above directions to
the restaurant.
Cuisine
This chef-owned restaurant serves simple, authentic
Asian food using seasonal and local ingredients.

Chef Andrea Reusing first experienced the magic of food and the
relationship a cook can have with purveyors when her grandmother took
her to market in Pennsylvania. She grew up in New Jersey and went to

Andrea Reusing

New York University, where she studied filmmaking. In New York, she also experienced the extraordinary dishes of Chinatown.

Though she came to North Carolina to be with her boyfriend, not to cook, her first job was in the brand-new Enoteca Vin in Raleigh, where she developed a following and the desire to open her own restaurant. While Andrea was at Enoteca Vin, she worked with upcoming chef Ashley Christensen, who now owns Poole's Downtown Diner in Raleigh.

Lantern opened its doors in 2002 in a storefront on West Franklin Street in Chapel Hill. Since then, it has attracted the attention of numerous national publications. *Gourmet* featured Andrea in its October 2008 issue, devoting fourteen pages to her recipes. The magazine ranks *Lantern* as one of the fifty best restaurants in the nation.

Andrea features the freshest local ingredients in her Asian style of cooking. She creates memorable and remarkable flavors. A strong advocate of using the products of local farmers, she is involved in the Slow Food movement. Slow Food International is a nonprofit, eco-gastronomic member-supported organization founded in 1989 to counteract fast food and the fast life. The Triangle's participation is one of the nation's largest and most active.

National publications including the *Wall Street Journal, Food & Wine,* the *New York Times, Saveur,* and others regularly feature Chef Andrea and Lantern. A semifinalist for the 2009 James Beard Award for Best Chef in the Southeast, she is currently working on a cookbook that will feature her home cooking.

Dorette Snover's
Mother Sauces

Chef Dorette Snover is the owner of C'est Si Bon! Cooking School in Chapel Hill. She is an expert on French culinary techniques and their history.

BASIL BÉCHAMEL

"Béchamel is 1 of 2 creamy mother sauces. The béchamel uses an onion *pique*—an onion that has a bay leaf nailed into it with a few whole cloves. The other creamy sauce, velouté, uses stock instead of milk. But both are thickened with a roux," Chef Dorette says.

Yields 2 cups

4 tablespoons butter
4 tablespoons flour
2½ cups half-and-half
1 large sweet onion, peeled and quartered
4 bay leaves
4 whole cloves
1 sprig fresh thyme
4 or 5 fresh basil leaves
Nutmeg, freshly grated
Salt and white pepper to taste

Make a roux by melting butter in a large, heavy saucepan over low heat and stirring in the flour until there are no lumps. Cook over low heat for a few minutes, stirring frequently.

In a separate saucepan, bring half-and-half to a boil with onion, bay leaves, cloves, thyme, basil, nutmeg, salt, and white pepper. Remove from heat and cover. Let mixture infuse for about 10 minutes.

Strain half-and-half into roux in its original pan. Mix. Bring to a boil, then simmer gently for 15 to 20 minutes. Adjust thickness by adding half-and-half to thin or by cooking a little longer to thicken.

This is a good sauce to pour over 4 cups of buttered pasta. Add ½ cup grated Parmesan, mix, and bake pasta at 350 degrees for 20 to 30 minutes until golden brown.

Shrimp and Scallop Classic Velouté

Serves 4

3 tablespoons butter
12 medium shrimp, shelled and deveined
6 sea scallops
Salt and freshly ground pepper to taste
2 teaspoons chopped shallots
2 teaspoons chopped garlic
1 cup sliced white mushrooms
3 tablespoons flour
1 cup white wine
Juice of 1 lemon
1 quart fumet (fish stock; can be made with shrimp shells)
1 pint heavy cream
4 teaspoons fresh parsley, chopped
4 teaspoons fresh chives, chopped

Melt butter in a sauté pan over medium-high heat, then sauté shrimp and scallops. Season with salt and pepper. Remove from pan and keep warm. Add a bit more butter to the pan if necessary, then add shallots, garlic, and mushrooms. Sauté until shallots are translucent, then add flour and combine until flour is absorbed. Deglaze with wine. Place lemon juice in another pan and pour in fumet. Cook for a few minutes over low heat until mixture reduces. Add cream and reduce over medium heat. Add butter-flour mixture and stir until everything starts to thicken. Season with salt and pepper.

Add scallops and shrimp and warm through. Serve over pasta or rice. Sprinkle parsley and chives on top.

HOLLANDAISE WITH ORANGE GINGER

"The basic method for this sauce comes from a tome of recipes, Auguste Escoffier's *Le Guide Culinaire*. Shuffling through this volume will give tremendous insight into the vast culinary work brought forth from the latter part of the 1800s and the early segments of the 1900s, works by the great Carême, Dubois, and Bernard," Chef Dorette says. "I like to make the hollandaise over direct heat. It takes a bit more care when making, but when you're done, you're done. No double boilers to fuss with or to wash. I love that, and you might, too."

Yields approximately 1½ cups

3 teaspoons wine or vinegar
Pinch of salt
3 egg yolks
1 cup plus 2 tablespoons butter, melted
1 to 2 teaspoons fresh orange juice
1 to 2 teaspoons grated ginger
Salt and pepper to taste
Cayenne pepper to taste

Place wine or vinegar in a stainless-steel bowl with a pinch of salt and whisk over medium heat until reduced by ⅔. Remove bowl from heat to cool a bit. Add yolks to pan and whisk continuously over gentle heat until yolks are thickened and light yellow. Your whisk will leave a trail through yolks. Gradually add melted butter. Add orange juice and ginger. Add salt, pepper, and cayenne. Serve over roasted or blanched asparagus.

Recipe Index